'This ground-breaking book venture: reviewing and synthesising insights from many sources. Going beyond t consciousness, David Fontana boldly journey and destination, coaxing readers beyond their limited conceptions. A must-read for those seriously interested in the meaning and purpose of life.'

DAVID LORIMER
Programme Director of the Scientific and Medical Network

'This is a most valuable book, assembling as it does concepts of the nature of the afterlife, made more so by the fact that it is written by a psychologist and psychical researcher of great practical experience and perception. It should be read by many who, in this world of increasing troubles and secular pessimism, seek enlightenment, comfort and hope.'

ARCHIE E. ROY
Emeritus Professor, Glasgow University, Past President of the Society for Psychical Research, Founding President of the Scottish Society for Psychical Research, and Myers Memorial Medallist

A Selection of Books by David Fontana

Is There an Afterlife?
Psychology, Religion and Spirituality
Creative Meditation and Visualization
The New Secret Language of Dreams
The Meditator's Handbook
The Secret Language of Symbols
Learn to Meditate

DAVID FONTANA is a Professor of Psychology, Past President of the Society for Psychical Research, and a Fellow of the British Psychological Society. He has been investigating the evidence for survival of death for more than 40 years, and has written and lectured widely on the subject in Britain and abroad. The author of over 40 books that have been translated into 26 languages, he chairs the Survival Research Committee of the Society for Psychical Research. Among his recent books are *Is There an Afterlife?*, *Psychology Religion and Spirituality*, and *The New Secret Language of Dreams*. He considers that the question of survival of death and of the nature of survival is crucial to our understanding of who we are and why we are here.

LIFE
BEYOND
DEATH

WHAT SHOULD WE EXPECT?

David Fontana

WATKINS PUBLISHING

LONDON

Distributed in the United States and Canada by
Sterling Publishing Co., Inc.
387 Park Avenue South, New York, NY 10016-8810

This edition first published in the UK and USA 2009 by
Watkins Publishing, Sixth Floor, Castle House,
75–76 Wells Street, London w1t 3qh

1 3 5 7 9 10 8 6 4 2

Designed and typeset by Paul Saunders
Printed and bound in Great Britain

Library of Congress Cataloging-in-Publication data available

isbn: 978-1-906787-08-0

www.watkinspublishing.co.uk

For information about custom editions, special sales, premium and
corporate purchases, please contact Sterling Special Sales
Department at 800-805-5489 or specialsales@sterlingpub.com

CONTENTS

For Professor Archie Roy and Patricia Robertson
of the Scottish Society for Psychical Research, outstanding
researchers into survival of death, and wise and
generous friends.

Chapter One

·

THE MYSTERY OF THE AFTERLIFE

Curiosity and belief

I have always been fascinated by the deeper mysteries of life. Even as a very young boy I remember pondering about the next world. At church there was talk of heaven for those who lived a good life, and a darker place for the wicked, but beyond this broad division the details were few and far between. When I was a little older and started seeking to fill some of the gaps, adults gave me the distinct impression that everything should be left to faith. For me this didn't remove the mystery. What would the next life actually be *like*? What would we do with our time? Would we meet old friends and family again? Where would we live? Would there be new things to learn? Whatever adults thought, it seemed to me that these were legitimate questions. After all, we were told at school that questions were the sign of an enquiring mind.

As the years of childhood passed, I was surprised to find that curiosity about the next world was strangely lacking amongst most people, many of whom even seemed to have no belief in its existence. This lack of curiosity on the one hand, and of belief on the other, puzzled me. Weren't people intuitively aware of some

1

quality in themselves, call it a soul, that was not part of the physical world? It seemed clear to me that existence must be much more than the passing moments of our time-haunted lives on earth – which brought me back time and time again to the question of an afterlife and of a soul that lived on after death. The more I thought about the soul the more I thought about the mind, which seemed to me central to the soul because like the soul it seemed non-physical, full of non-physical things like consciousness, thoughts and memories. If the soul lived on, then presumably so did the mind, and if the mind lived on this meant we carried our consciousness, our thoughts and our memories and everything else that made up the mind, with us to the next world. The more I pondered these things, the more I came up against the fact that life was a very mysterious business. What a miracle it was that we should exist at all, that we should actually be alive! And what anyway *was* this strange thing called life? Life, soul and mind all seemed non-physical and inextricably linked with each other. So where did they go after leaving the physical body? Which brought me back time and again to my original question, what would the afterlife be *like*?

My interest in such things was one of the reasons why, in due course, I became a psychologist, since I assumed that psychology was about the mind and just possibly also had something to say about the soul (since the term 'psychology' in fact derives from *pukhe*, the Greek word for soul). I soon realized my mistake. Psychology has taught me a great deal about the brain, and about human behaviour, emotions, personality and much more besides. For 40 years I have been in love with the subject and my love is as strong as ever. But as with all branches of science its approach is firmly based in the physical world, and as such it can only take us so far. Science and the scientific method pause before non-physical realities such as mind and the soul. Science studies the brain, which is a physical organ, but the assumption that the mind is no more than a function of the brain and therefore also physical is just that, an assumption. Certainly when the mind is active there are electrical changes in the brain, but electrical changes are not the mind. Similarly there are chemical changes, but chemical changes are not the mind. Attempts to dismiss the mind as nothing more than a function of the brain are in fact based upon the presupposition that mind is a function of the brain, and presuppositions are not evidence. Mind and brain certainly interact, just as a television signal interacts with the electrical circuitry in a television set, but this does not mean the brain causes the mind or that the mind dies when the brain dies, any more than the electrical circuitry in the television set causes the signal or that when the television set is destroyed so is the signal.

And if the mind resists attempts to treat it as a physical organ how much more does the soul. So, to the sceptic who insists that thanks to science we 'know' there is no such thing as a soul or an afterlife I would reply that we 'know' no such thing. This point will be touched on several times in the book but let us be clear from the outset that since science deals with the world of physical matter it has nothing to say as yet on what comes afterwards. Certainly there are interesting developments in science (particularly in quantum physics) that suggest that not only is matter a form of energy, but that matter and mind may be part of a continuum that links the physical world with the non-physical dimension of consciousness, even that mind and matter may both be expression of the one underlying reality (*see* Goswami et al 1993 and Goswami 2002 for excellent introductions to this field). But far from suggesting that mind is merely a by-product of matter, these developments seem to point in the opposite direction, namely that matter may be a product of mind. And far from serving to weaken the case for survival of physical death they can actually be interpreted as strengthening it.

However, even work of this kind has nothing to tell us about the *nature* of a possible afterlife, and we must leave it at that; for the present at least, science effectively stops short with the fact of death itself. Incidentally, this is perhaps the point at which to say that as my concern in the present book is with what comes after death I shall not have space to say much about the evidence for survival *per se*, although I must make it clear that when studied with the care it deserves, this evidence shows that belief in survival of death has strong support, as I have attempted to show in a previous book, *Is There an Afterlife?* (Fontana 2005).

Source material

For anyone who writes about the afterlife there are many pitfalls. How does one approach a subject that may involve concepts for which we have no adequate language, and that touch on many of the most cherished ideas and beliefs of readers? And when selecting material to include how does one decide what seems reliable and what does not? We cannot send volunteers into the next world and then bring them back to tell us what they have discovered (although, as we shall see in due course, so-called 'near-death experiences' bring us close to this). And when individuals claim to have received communications from the next world, through mediums or through seeing visions or apparitions, how much weight can we attach to these claims, especially as the fact that we may want the departed to contact us can leave us very vulnerable to wishful thinking and self-deception? Mediumship, through which the majority of these contacts come, must obviously be approached with caution. Some mediums receive their communications in a state of trance, while others remain fully conscious and a very few are associated with the physical materialization of the deceased. However, even if the evidence produced by these various means is accurate and free from possibilities of trickery, we still have to ask if the communicating entities really are who they say they are. Are their personalities consistent with those of the individuals they claim to have been before death? Do they give truthful information that could not have been known to the medium? In the present book we will only draw on material from mediums whose contacts with the deceased are known on good authority to have passed these tests, and whose information is likely to be informative on the afterlife (the great majority of material received through mediums tends rather disappointingly to concern this world rather than the next).

Other important sources of material available to us include reports of near-death experiences (experiences of those who have been briefly at or near clinical death), of the dying themselves, and of some of the great spiritual traditions (although space only allows us to draw in any detail upon Christianity and Buddhism). The Western mystery (or 'occult' or 'esoteric' – words simply meaning 'hidden') traditions dating back to the ancient Greeks also have something to tell us. We may prefer certain of these sources to others, but there is an interesting level of consistency between the information they each give. We must remember of course that if an afterlife exists it is a different reality from the material world, even though it might appear to resemble the latter, and that we cannot critically appraise information on it as we appraise information within our own reality. All we can do is to judge it by the agreement between the various relevant accounts, by their credibility and by our appraisal of the sources themselves.

I make no excuse for drawing some of the evidence provided by mediumship and the experiences of the dying from material first reported some years ago. Evidence stands or falls by its quality not by its age, and some of the best mediums of all time were working in the years between the two world wars, when people had more time and inclination to develop mediumistic gifts. The belief that things are only of value if they are modern is unfair to the past and to readers intent on obtaining a comprehensive picture of the subject.

Difficulty with terms

Terms present as many difficulties as sources. When we mention the departed should we call them 'souls' or 'spirits' or 'entities' or 'the deceased'? Should we use terms like 'earthbound' for those who, after death, are said to remain close to earth or does this suggest we are surrounded with disembodied phantoms? Should we use words like 'Hades', 'astral', 'paradise' or 'heaven' when talking about various levels of the afterlife, or does this suggest we are into the occult or preaching religion? All the available terms have become so misunderstood and misused as to have all sorts of confusing connotations. Even terms for paranormal abilities such as 'telepathy' and 'clairvoyance' and 'mediumship' are now suspect in many quarters. Thus, although I have to use these various terms for want of anything better I do so with reservations, and my use of them does not necessarily imply a belief in all the things for which they may stand. To avoid tedium I shall not always use cautious words like 'supposed', 'claimed', 'alleged', 'seemingly', and when these are omitted they must be understood. However, whenever I do make use of them it does not imply that the book is based on mere conjecture. If it were it would not be worth writing. Much of what is said adds up to a coherent and consistent view of the afterlife based on sources that may make sense to all those who do not on principle dismiss any possibility that we live on after death. Those who dismiss the possibility are unlikely to read this book anyway, and it is not for me to tell them how best to use their time.

Conclusion

I have been studying the evidence for the afterlife in the vast literature on the subject and through my own research for nearly 40 years. In view of the volume of information available it is not possible to cover everything in the number of words available to me. Inevitably some readers will query why nothing has been said of their own favourite pieces of evidence, and I can only plead pressures of space. I am only too well aware of the additional material I would like to include but which has fallen victim to these pressures. I am also aware that any book on the afterlife risks being criticized on the one hand for being too cautious about its nature and on the other for being too ready to accept its reality, but that is inevitable with any book on such a controversial subject. My aim is to present a selection of the information available to us, and then leave it to readers to make their own assessment of its value.

Finally, to those who feel anxiety at any mention of death and a possible afterlife I should like to say that avoiding these subjects only tells our unconscious we are afraid of them, which serves to increase our fear. Studying them helps reduce our fear, and in the process takes us a step closer to understanding the deepest mystery of all, the mystery of our own being. As physicist and astronomer Dr David Darling (1995) points out, once the fear of death and of what comes after death has been removed by the knowledge that consciousness continues, 'our whole outlook on caring for the dying will be permanently transformed ... The dying will be allowed to slip away quietly, peacefully, joyfully. And we can wish them well on the voyage ahead.'

A Note on References

When the work of other named authors is referred to from time to time they are followed by a date, which allows the reader to locate the relevant references at the end of the book. This is the usual practice adopted by authors, and avoids having to interrupt the text by printing full book titles on every occasion.

Chapter Two

.

NEAR DEATH AND ACTUAL DEATH

The moment of passing

When we lose someone close to us we find ourselves wondering if their experience, their hopes, their wisdom and their love for others have all come to nothing. Have they vanished except for a handful of ashes or a tombstone in a silent churchyard? Even if we believe in an afterlife we may be left wondering what is happening to the departed and what awaits them at their destination. Such questions are natural enough. If we were watching a friend depart for a far country or if we were leaving for a far country ourselves we would want to ask similar things. The wise traveller always prepares properly for a journey, knowing this will ease the path that lies ahead. And if this is true for travellers in this world, how much more may it be true for travellers in the next.

Nevertheless, some people claim that an interest in the afterlife distracts attention from the here and now. The opposite is true. The great spiritual traditions all emphasize not only that the present life cannot be understood unless seen in the context of a future existence, but that certain social and moral behaviour is necessary in this life if we are to be properly prepared for the wider horizons of the next. The majority of the world's population share the belief in an afterlife of some sort, and this is even true of secular Westerners, but believing in something and knowing the implications it has for how we live our lives are two different things.

Events on the threshold

The place to start a study of the afterlife is with death itself and with what it might be like to die, and some of the evidence for this comes from near-death experiences (NDEs). The term NDE refers to those incidents when individuals are near or actually clinically dead (i.e. briefly with no measurable heart or brain activity). Modern methods of resuscitation mean that many people are now brought back from this twilight state, and a number of researchers have recorded the accounts given by people of what this state is actually like (*see* Crookall 1978, Moody 1977, Fenwick and Fenwick 1995, Fox 2003). If these accounts were of only a blank nothingness this would argue against the existence of an afterlife. However, a significant percentage – for example 12 per cent of the 344 cardiac arrest cases studied by Dr Van Lommel and colleagues at Rijnstate Hospital in the Netherlands (Van Lommel et al 2001) – report a continuation of consciousness experienced as outside the physical body. Even among a randomly chosen sample of 1,000 UK residents Dr Sam Parnia (Parnia 2005) found that 10 per cent reported having also experienced being outside their bodies, either in an NDE or while in normal health (referred to as an OBE or out-of-the-body experience).

Here is an example given by Dr Robert Crookall, whose many books are a mine of case studies of such experiences. The account concerned is a brief one, but compelling in its simplicity and honesty and very representative of many such cases. It comes from a young woman who was pronounced dead while giving birth.

I heard the doctor say 'Well, she's dead! I must tell her husband!' Meanwhile I had left my body and felt myself floating in what seemed like a dark tunnel (with a glimpse, at the end, of a lovely countryside). I had no pain, only a wonderful feeling of happiness. I felt I had somebody with me, but saw nobody. Only I heard a voice which said 'You must go back! The child needs you!' I returned to my body and heard the doctor say 'No, by Jove, I can still feel her heart!' This experience convinced me of a future world after death and gave me an everlasting faith.

It is interesting to see how accounts such as this, written some years ago, agree in details with those written today. For example, in one of the accounts published by Parnia from a woman whose heart had stopped during a hysterectomy, the subject speaks of 'whizzing through a dark tunnel', of seeing a 'blinding bright light at the end of it', of emerging into 'a beautiful meadow', and of meeting a young woman wearing a white dress who 'kept telling me that I must go back, that it was too soon for me to be there and that there were things I had to do still in my life. I felt quite bereft ... but remembered that I had three children ... '. The individual in one of the accounts published in her excellent review and discussion of the NDE experience by Margot Grey (1985) also describes the tunnel experience and continues:

> you may be reaching the end of the tunnel as you can see a white light ... Gradually as you travel towards it ... it gets larger and larger ... before you is this magnificent, beautiful blue-white light that ... absolutely does not hurt your eyes at all.

Other accounts quoted by Grey also include references to this light and to a beautiful countryside. For example:

> The experience ... was total beauty ... The light was extremely bright but it wasn't a harsh light ... I ... felt absolute peace ...

All I know is that I was there, I'm not afraid of it ... it's something beautiful beautiful.

The above accounts contain between them several characteristics typical of NDEs, i.e. the ability to hear the diagnosis of clinical death, the feeling of floating into a dark tunnel, the glimpse of bright light and then of a lovely countryside at the end of the tunnel, the absence of pain, the feeling of happiness, the instruction to return to the body, and the lasting conviction of a life after death. This conviction is one of the best testimonies to the enduring psychological effect of the NDE. The majority of those who report NDEs claim their experiences have removed any fear of death – they have died once and know what it is like. In his investigations Dr Michael Sabom found that 82 per cent of his NDE sample claimed to have been left with a reduced fear of death, while 77 per cent claimed an increased belief in an afterlife. By comparison, only 2 per cent of those in a sample of patients who had *not* had an NDE during their clinical death reported a reduction in their fear, and none reported increased belief in an afterlife. Interestingly, there were no differences in religious affiliations between those in Sabom's samples who had NDEs and those who did not, suggesting that religious expectation did not influence NDE occurrence (Sabom 1982 and 1998).

But could NDEs be hallucinations?

Critics have claimed that NDEs may simply be hallucinations caused by medical drugs, or by anoxia (lack of oxygen) or hypercarbia (carbon build-up in the blood), and therefore tell us nothing about dying or an afterlife. However, this claim has been answered by a number of authorities on brain and mind such as neuropsychiatrist Peter Fenwick of the University of London's Maudsley Hospital (Fenwick and Fenwick 1995). In a study of 300

NDE cases Fenwick found that only 14 per cent were receiving drugs at the time of their NDEs – and points out that in any case drug-induced hallucinations are random and disorganized in contrast to NDE experiences, which are typically vivid and coherent. Fenwick also dismisses anoxia on the grounds that although the condition is regularly induced in airline pilots as part of their training (and also at one time in medical students), none of those involved appears to have reported an NDE. In addition, anoxia leads to brain disorientation and confusion. He agrees that hypercarbia can prompt hallucinations, but it also produces convulsive muscle movements which are not present in NDE patients. The argument that NDEs are caused by endorphins, the brain's own pain-killing drugs, is also unconvincing, since NDE-type experiences are not reported by groups experiencing high endorphin levels such as long-distance runners.

An argument also sometimes put forward is that NDEs may be caused by anomalies in brain electricity, since stimulating certain brain areas with weak electrical currents can produce mystical-type experiences, but again these experiences tend to be disorganized and fragmentary, unlike the integrated and meaningful experiences typical of NDEs. Furthermore, those reporting NDEs are not receiving brain stimulation at the time. The argument that NDEs are similar to experiences under psychedelic drugs such as LSD and mescaline also ignores the fact that, unlike the consistent, unifying features of NDEs, these drug experiences are typically intensely personal in nature and vary sharply from individual to individual (*see* Groff 1975). However, the classified drug ketamine, used medically as a dissociative anaesthetic (an anaesthetic that produces sensory loss but without loss of consciousness), does sometimes prompt apparent out-of-the-body experiences when used in subclinical doses. In a recent study of 36 ketamine users Ornella Corazza (2008) found that some 33 per cent of her sample insisted they were 'absolutely sure' that when under the influence of the drug they were out of their bodies and in some cases actually saw their bodies from an external viewpoint. There were also reports of tunnel experiences, of meetings with angelic beings and with the deceased, and of visiting mystical domains – many of the characteristics of NDEs. Such visions were markedly less frequent than in NDEs, but nevertheless 46 per cent of those questioned by Corazza reported a reduced fear of death as a result of their ketamine experiences.

Ketamine is not used clinically with those approaching death so cannot be offered as an explanation for reported NDE experiences, but why should it nevertheless mimic some of these experiences? One suggestion is that ketamine may have chemical effects upon the brain similar to those possibly taking place during NDEs, but irrespective of whether this is correct or not, ketamine may inhibit those areas of the brain that usually prevent the mind from losing contact with the body. Thus it may facilitate the conditions under which out-of-body experiences can take place (which is obviously not the same thing as actually causing them). Karl Jansen (2001), although not particularly sympathetic to an other-dimensional interpretation of ketamine experiences, accepts that among other possibilities ketamine may allow the mind to 'connect' to other realities, though he rightly points out the dangers of its use for this purpose.

A further attempt to explain NDEs by critics is that the brain is dying and becoming chaotic at the time and losing peripheral imagery (hence the tunnel effect). However, if NDEs are the result of the dying brain we would expect them to become increasingly incoherent, whereas the NDE typically becomes *more* coherent as it progresses. The claim that loss of peripheral vision causes the tunnel experience fails to explain why some individuals report coming to the end of the tunnel and entering a beautiful landscape, or why some individuals report the tunnel effect reoccurring briefly during their *return* to the body, when the brain would presumably no longer be dying.

Another claim is that those who report NDEs are influenced

by what they have read. However, when questioned on their prior knowledge of NDEs the overwhelming number of individuals report they knew nothing about the phenomenon. In addition, investigators do not mention NDEs before listening to the accounts given by those with the experience, and simply ask if they remember anything of the time when they lost consciousness during their medical emergencies. Of course, we have to rely upon people's honesty, but Dr Melvin Morse (Morse and Perry 1990) found that 8 out of 12 children whose medical records showed they had experienced cardiac arrest, reported NDEs very similar to those of adults, and there was no evidence that at their young age they even knew that NDEs existed.

Are individuals who experience NDEs really dead?

This depends upon what we mean by death. As individuals reporting NDEs have been successfully resuscitated, have they really died? The short answer is that all those in Dr Pim Van Lommel's study referenced earlier, and in many other studies, were pronounced clinically dead. In addition, those who have NDEs typically insist they *know* they have died, and in the great majority of cases their attitude to life and to its goals and values and to spiritual realities become significantly more positive. By all recognized criteria they have died and returned from death to bodies still capable of supporting life. Modern methods of resuscitation revive people who would have remained clinically dead a few years ago, but this gives us no justification for changing the goalposts on what is meant by clinical death. Clinical death is defined as the absence of the vital signals that support physical life, and there is nothing in this definition that says restoration of these physical signs demonstrates that clinical death could not have taken place. Medically, it may be that the boundary between life and death can be briefly crossed in both directions by the sick, and that this is what happens in the NDE.

Even the argument that people from different cultures report significantly different NDEs is not sustainable. Osis and Haraldsson (1995), in a four-year study in the USA and India involving 877 detailed interviews with terminally ill patients, concluded that the 120 who reported NDEs had had a core experience common to both cultures, and that this core experience is one of the most revealing factors of the NDE supporting the possibility of survival of death. In addition they noted that a number of the contrasting basic beliefs present in the predominant religions of both cultures – such as external judgement, salvation and redemption in the case of Christians and reincarnation and dissolution into Brahman in the case of Hindus – were notably absent, a fact that allowed them to assert that cultural conditioning by Christian and Hindu teachings is not apparent in all 'the visionary experiences of the dying'. Furthermore, although religious belief is very much a feature of both US and Indian cultures, 'the phenomena within [the samples studied in] each culture often did not conform to religious afterlife beliefs'.

What do NDEs tell us about dying?

We listed some of the characteristics of the NDE after the example above of the woman who 'died' in childbirth, and many others emerge from the many cases in the literature. Firstly, some individuals report watching from a position outside their bodies at the medical team trying to revive them, and even repeat some of the words that were spoken, which suggests that once free of their bodies the dying may remain at least briefly in their physical surroundings. Secondly, after the tunnel experience, some individuals actually report entering the beautiful landscape mentioned earlier where they meet deceased friends or family or 'beings of light' who send them back or give them a choice to stay or return. Thirdly, there is frequent reference to returning to the body with great reluctance, drawn back only by thoughts of loved ones or of unfinished work. Fourthly, re-entry into the physical body is often described as very distasteful, like being drawn into a mass of cold clay or icy water. Only in a small minority of cases is the NDE described as unpleasant (more of this later).

NDEs came to popular attention in 1997 with the publication by Dr Raymond Moody of *Life After Life*, but in fact they are reported much earlier than this. Probably the earliest account we have is from the 4th century BCE when Plato mentions that a Greek soldier called Er was pronounced dead but recovered while awaiting cremation and described having left his body and travelled to a strange country accompanied by other soldiers who had also died with him, only to be eventually sent back to his body. F W H Myers, in his classic *Human Personality and its Survival of Bodily Death* (1903) also refers to early examples. The significant point is that, as with Crookall's cases mentioned earlier, these various examples were published before the appearance of Moody's book and the modern interest in NDEs, and thus could not have been influenced by them. Yet they tell very similar stories.

However, this does not mean that intriguing apparent idiosyncrasies do not sometimes occur. A description by one of Michael Sabom's patients begins typically enough. He describes how, while unconscious in hospital after a road accident, he saw his body and everything in the room from a position some way above. He saw the screen of the heart monitor show an absence of heart activity, and watched doctors thumping his chest, then administering electric shocks to the heart, which made his body 'jump' some inches from the operating table. At this point he found himself making his way in darkness towards a distant bright light that, when he reached it, proved to be a beautiful blue colour – 'I've never seen a blue like that' – he was then surrounded by his six children. Now comes the idiosyncrasy. All six children were *still alive on earth.* Stranger still, in the NDE the children were 'all almost the same age', around six years old. His impression was that this age represented the most enjoyable period he had had with each of the children.

> I remembered ... tea parties with [my oldest daughter] when she was a little girl ... My older boy I remember ... building a bookcase and he was talking to me about something he wanted to do ... [it was] the most favourite, the most intimate time I had had with them. Something with each of them that had struck me personally.'

He then felt a pressure on his head and heard a voice say 'Go back', to which he replied 'Why me Lord?', and was told that his work on earth wasn't over yet, and that he had to go back and complete it. The voice was 'loud, thundering', and the next thing he knew he was waking up in intensive care two days later.

Critics will judge that this episode with the six children shows the whole experience was pure imagination. But such a judgement is premature. As we shall see in Chapter 6, accounts of the events surrounding death and NDEs sometimes include what is called a 'life review', an experience in which the past life of the individual flashes before him, rapidly, yet somehow giving ample time for each event and its meaning and emotional impact to register. The fact that each child appeared to be around six years old and the patient was reminded of the most intimate and enjoyable period he had had with him or her suggests that they were a fragment of this review. The life review does not always go in chronological order, and in this case it seemed to start with the children. Most fathers reading of this experience will readily identify with it. As fathers we have all had these deeply moving intimate times with our children when they were small, and these times are often among the most precious experiences of our lives.

If space allowed we could go on giving examples of NDEs – I

have revealing accounts in my own files given to me by those personally involved. But let's summarize what has been said so far of the various stages involved.

Stage 1 Individuals, either near death or clinically dead, find their consciousness located outside the physical body. Sometimes they see their physical body on the ground or the operating table and observe the activities of the people attending to it. There is a sense of detachment from the body and there is no consciousness of pain or suffering.

Stage 2 Subsequently (or sometimes immediately on leaving the body) there is often a sensation of entering a dark 'tunnel' with a bright light in the distance.

Stage 3 On reaching the light there is awareness of beautiful surroundings and perhaps of meeting spiritual beings or deceased relatives or friends.

Stage 4 A choice may be given of staying or of returning to the body, or a command given to return.

Stage 5 The consciousness is drawn back to the body and enters it, usually with reluctance or repugnance. Sensations of physical pain may once more be felt.

Stage 6 The conviction remains that death has been experienced, and the fear of death disappears or is greatly reduced.

Not everyone goes through all six stages. Some only reach Stage 1 before returning to the body. Sometimes he or she may miss out (or have no memory of) the tunnel, and go straight to Stages 3 and 4. But typically the act of leaving the body seems easy, as if death itself is rather like shedding an unwanted garment. I have found nothing in the literature on NDEs to suggest the actual *act* of leaving the body is difficult or painful, and the same may generally be true when death finally occurs. In the latter instance the individual may appear to be fighting for breath or showing extreme agitation but such things, particularly if the patient is unconscious, are said by the deceased communicating through mediums to be purely reflex physical actions rather than actual distress. Exceptions can be individuals who refuse to accept death and struggle against it to the last. Even for them, however, communicators tell us the actual moment of passing remains painless. The soul does not tear itself away from the body. Some communicators speak of death as a progressive process, as if the body shuts down its various functions starting with the feet and culminating in the crown, while others report being lifted out of their bodies and remaining suspended above them until the 'silken cord' said to connect the soul to the body finally breaks (more of this in the next chapter). Furthermore, except for those who die a sudden death, the immediate after-death experience also seems usually to be peaceful. The individual looks back unemotionally at the discarded body, and feels no regret at leaving it.

We do not know if some of those who are offered the choice (referred to in Stage 4 above) of returning from an NDE reject it, thus rendering death permanent. Obviously, return is only possible if the body remains capable of supporting life, which is usually the case for only a short while after clinical death. In the last days of life, terminally ill people may in fact briefly drift in and out of their bodies during periods of unconsciousness, returning only as long as the body remains viable. Those suffering from dementia may find themselves unable to make use of the disabled areas of their brains or to communicate coherently, though remaining fully conscious behind the veil of their disability. Some support for this possibility comes from experienced nurses who have assured me that even profoundly unconscious patients have, upon recovery, sometimes reported being fully aware of what was said and done around them even when they were comatose. If so, then consciousness can perhaps be fully operational even when the body refuses to respond to its promptings or to give any indication of its existence.

Unpleasant NDE experiences

So far I have presented a positive picture of NDEs, but some reports of unpleasant NDEs have been published by Professor Bruce Greyson of the University of Virginia (Greyson and Flynn 1984, Greyson and Bush 1992) and by George Gallup (1983). Such unpleasant experiences, though rare, seem to be of three types. In the first type the NDE starts in the typical way, but the individual then becomes alarmed that he or she may be dead and returns rapidly to the physical body, sometimes with the help of a spiritual being. In the second the individual finds himself in a featureless void and may hear mocking voices saying that this is all there is for the whole of eternity, and that everything previously learnt about life after death is a cruel joke. In the third type the individual, although not personally undergoing any suffering and even in the safe company of higher beings, is alarmed to hear the cries and moans of those who appear to be experiencing torments of some kind.

The first type of negative experience obviously suggests a particularly strong fear of death. Reports of OBEs from healthy individuals whose consciousness is abruptly and unexpectedly located outside their bodies (*see* Buhlman 1996 and Peterson 1997) indicate that fear prompts a rapid return, and fear may have similar consequences in an NDE. The second type of experience may result from the state of mind in which the individual has 'died'. Eastern and Western spiritual traditions both emphasize the importance of this state for determining the immediate post-mortem experience, with agitation, fear and confusion leading to negative experiences (*see* Storm 2000), and we have more to say on this later. The third type of experience perhaps supports the belief that suffering is indeed possible in the afterlife, a possibility explored in Chapter 6.

An account of an NDE containing the second type of experience comes from the famous 1970s French movie star Daniel Gélin. Taken to hospital after suffering a heart attack in 1971, Gélin was conscious of the doctor pronouncing him dead, and of the nurse covering his face with a sheet. Terrified and unable to move or speak, he made repeated but futile attempts to alert the staff to the fact he was still alive. Subsequently, finding himself outside his body, he 'reached a point of great despair and aloneness … the emptiness in which I now found myself trapped was horrible'. However, realizing he had become 'light and insubstantial', he was aware that his movements were stirring up 'a cloud of gleaming dust', and that the sky was like a preternaturally clear and very light blue dome 'that seemed pure and transparent'. He then found himself surrounded by 'shadows and shapes' among which he recognized his deceased parents, who gradually became clear to him ('it was an unimaginable miracle for me to find [them] again under the great sun of a happy hereafter'). He also met his son who had died in adolescence, before hearing his mother telling him sadly 'Go now Daniel, it's time, life is waiting.' Gélin put up a fierce battle against returning to the living. 'I wanted to stay where I was. I ranted and raved like a madman … All in vain. An inexorable force bore me away … I was lost in a boundless world without light and colour.' He then found himself back in his body and in excruciating pain. 'My head was filled with a yawning emptiness.' (Delacour 1974)

Negative NDE experiences may be less common among people with religious belief since research indicates that such people, when terminally ill, face death with greater serenity and acceptance than people without belief (Koenig et al 2001). The last rites administered to the dying by the priest are intended to facilitate this serenity and acceptance, and in addition, both

Eastern religions (Buddhism in particular) and Western mediumistic communications also stress that some knowledge of what to expect in the immediate afterlife plays a major role in helping avoid post-mortem fear and confusion.

Finally, what of those people who return from clinical death with nothing to report, positive or negative? Have they no afterlife, or is there an unconscious mechanism that prevents them from recalling their experience, perhaps because it may prove difficult for them to handle the profound psychological changes that can follow an NDE (this possibility could be tested by seeing if they recall these memories under hypnosis). Life values and life goals are often changed by an NDE, and individuals may grow distant from family and friends, abandon careers, become more spiritually inclined, and may even develop apparent psychic abilities (*see* Ring 1984). Perhaps, as the poet T S Eliot puts it, 'human kind cannot bear too much reality', and like a dream that fades before waking the NDE is repressed and forgotten. However, even if this is not so, we still have to ask where was their consciousness during the brief period of apparent brain death? In the body or out of the body?

How similar are NDEs to actual death?

The evidence that NDEs involve the consciousness briefly leaving the physical body and surviving in a disembodied state is strong enough to be taken seriously, as is the possibility that the experience may provide us with insights into the immediate afterlife. We can now look at reports of the moment of death received by mediums, apparently from the deceased, in order to note any similarities. Here are two examples from Crookall (1978), followed by one from another highly respected investigator, Paul Beard (1980).

1. I saw about me those that had been dead for a long time ... Then I seemed to rise up and out of my body and come down quietly on the floor ... There seemed to be two of me, one on

the bed and one beside the bed ... I was gently told [by those who had died] what had happened.

2. I seemed to be lifted above the usual surroundings. I was ... with those who had passed over recently ... I was not conscious of any change or of anything abrupt ... I knew I was not on earth because of the long-lost people around me.

3. I suddenly found I was floating above my body ... Nothing in life comes close to the immense joy of dying ... I welcomed this inrush of new life and let go very willingly ... It's the most beautiful and glorious thing.

Other accounts published by Crookall and by Beard and others sometimes mention a door or an opening, or the tunnel mentioned in NDEs ('When I was dying there was a door ... in the corner of the room'; 'I remember a curious opening, as if one had passed through subterranean passages and found oneself near the mouth of a cave'). There are also references to an expansion of consciousness ('... I came out into a strange clearness'; 'I expanded in every direction, I was boundless, infinite'; 'the soul suddenly seems to expand'), and as with NDEs the emphasis is upon how easy everything is ('... my turn to make what some believe is a long journey. But for me it was such a short journey ... it was so incredibly easy and painless'; 'death is ... a mere episode which we regard with a certain tenderness and not with any pain'). Further examples of the experience of dying appear in the next chapter, but we can summarize the main similarities with NDEs that emerge from communications by the deceased and from observations actually made by the dying just before death.

- As with NDEs there is an awareness by the dying of their consciousness leaving the physical body. Sometimes the process is gradual, at others the consciousness is suddenly outside the body, often floating above it. As in NDEs, the consciousness is always described as pain free.

- Some communicators report that consciousness after death is in a body resembling the physical body (more of this in later chapters). This is also the case in many NDEs.

- Sometimes, as in NDEs, communicators report an awareness of the discarded physical body and of medical staff and mourners at the bedside.

- As in NDEs, the dying frequently refer to deceased relatives or friends who appear to be present.

- As with NDEs, communicators sometimes refer to a 'tunnel' or a 'door' or of entering a dark space with a distant 'light' towards which they are travelling.

- Communicators mention an 'expansion of consciousness' and/ or feelings of bliss commensurate with the reluctance shown by NDEers to return to their physical bodies.

- As with NDEs, communicators rarely express regret at leaving their bodies except for instances of sudden or violent death.

These similarities suggest that leaving the body is a simple, natural, painless process that enables consciousness to move on to new experiences. As with all human testimony, there are individual variations between reported accounts but these are outweighed by the consistencies, which suggests the existence of a unified core experience.

Unseen deathbed visitors

However, what of those individuals from whom nothing is heard after death? One possible answer is that, assuming the afterlife is universal, they may not have communicated because surviving friends and relatives have proved unreceptive to their efforts or have never visited mediums (many mediums do in fact claim to be almost overwhelmed by unknown souls clamouring to communicate, and to be forced to rely upon 'gatekeepers' or 'controls' in the spirit world to keep out those not relevant to sitters). Another possibility is that they may have no wish to communicate, or may have rapidly forgotten their earth lives. Early Greek traditions refer to a symbolic 'river of forgetfulness' from which souls drink after death (*see* Plato's *Timaeus*), and it is possible that once the second 'life review' discussed in Chapter 9 has been completed there is no further need to retain earth memories. But let us turn now to the experiences reported by some individuals just before death. Typically these involve seeing so-called 'deathbed visitors', usually deceased relatives or friends – who seem to come to help them make the transition to the afterlife.

When my mother was in her 90s, and failing in physical though not mental health, she asked me more than once for the identity of the 'other people' she could see in her bedroom. We were in fact alone on these occasions, but she insisted that on either side of her there were groups of people, supposedly visitors. It is important to allow people facing death to share their experiences, and I simply answered that I did not know. A few weeks nearer the end, but when she was still mentally alert and undrugged, she asked me who was the woman standing at the foot of her bed. She described her as dark-haired and youngish, although she could not recognize her. My mother's experiences were similar to many such events (incidentally she had never read anything of deathbed visitors and took little interest in psychical research). In 1926, physicist Sir William Barrett FRS, the inspiration along with Dawson Rogers behind the founding of the Society for Psychical Research (SPR), published *Death-Bed Visions* in which he described a number of these events. Since Barrett's book various other accounts of deathbed visions have been published, in many of which the unseen visitors have actually been recognized as deceased friends and family.

On occasions the dying person is reported as speaking to the visitors, and may even remark that they have come as helpers to show the way to the next world. The dying derive great comfort from these visions, which are occasionally also seen and recognized by mourners at the deathbed. At other times the visitors are seen in the form of mist or clouds. Here are examples of both types of experience quoted by Professor Barrett, the first given by Joy Snell, a nurse experienced in caring for the dying. and the second by Dr Rentz, a medical doctor.

> ... I was engaged to nurse ... Mrs Barton, aged 60, who was suffering from a painful internal disease ... a widow with an only daughter [who] lived with her... The time came when the end was very near... suddenly two [apparitions] became visible to me, standing on either side of the bed ... one was a man ... apparently about 60 years of age ... His beard and hair were iron-grey ... but ... on his feature ... that indescribable something indicative of exuberant vitality and vigour ... the other was a woman apparently ten or fifteen years younger ... The dying woman opened her eyes, and into them there came that look of glad recognition I have so often observed in those whose spirits are about to be released for ever ... She stretched forth her two hands ... One [apparition] grasped one hand and the other the other hand ... while their radiant faces were aglow with the joy of welcome. 'Oh Willie,' exclaimed Mrs Barton, 'you have come to take me home at last ... and you too Martha.' With the joyous light still in her eyes her hands remained outstretched for perhaps half a minute. Then they seemed to slip from her grasp. All her sufferings were over.

It seems unlikely that an experienced nurse, connected to the dying woman only in a professional capacity, could be thought to have hallucinated this experience as a result of grief. Moreover her descriptions of the two apparitions were subsequently recognized by the dead woman's daughter as those of her father and of an Aunt Martha, Mrs Barton's deceased sister.

The second example was related by Dr Rentz, a medical doctor attending a dying woman, Mrs G, together with her husband who informed Rentz he had had the following experience in the hours before his wife's death.

I happened to look towards the door when I saw floating through the doorway three separate and distinct clouds in strata ... [each] appeared to be about four feet in length, from six to eight inches in width ... Slowly these clouds approached the bed until they completely enveloped it. Then gazing through the mist I beheld standing at the head of my dying wife a woman's figure ...like a sheen of brightest gold ... so glorious in appearance that no words can fitly describe it ... dressed in a Grecian costume ... upon her head a brilliant crown ... the figure remained motionless with hands uplifted over my wife, seeming to express a welcome. Two figures in white knelt by my wife's side, apparently leaning towards her ... Above my wife, and connected with a cord from her forehead ... there floated in a horizontal position a nude, white figure, apparently her 'astral body' ... This vision, or whatever it may be called, I saw continuously during the five hours preceding the death of my wife ... At last the fatal moment arrived ...with a gasp, the astral figure struggling, my wife ceased to breathe ...With her last gasp, as the soul left the body, the cord was severed and the astral figure vanished. The clouds and the spirit forms disappeared instantly ... I was myself, cool, calm and deliberate ... I leave the reader to determine whether I was labouring under a mental delusion ... or if a glimpse of a spirit world ... was granted to my mortal eyes.

If we accept the possibility of an afterlife we will probably prefer the second explanation, particularly as unlike 'mental delusions' (hallucination) deathbed visions are typically coherent and meaningful. In reporting the incident Dr Rentz testifies that Mr G, 'was

in a perfectly normal state before and after [the experience], and
... there were features in the vision that would not have been likely
to occur to him'. Furthermore, Rentz insists he 'can most positively
put aside a temporary acute state of hallucinatory insanity during
the time of the vision ... I knew Mr G well and I had occasion to
know that he never read anything in the occult line; that everything that was not a proven fact was incompatible with his positive
mind ... [throughout the period of the vision] he was sitting
almost motionless next to her ...'.

Variations between 'visitors' who appear much as in life or who
seem to be in 'spiritualized' form may simply reflect the needs or
spiritual inclinations of the dying, with the former experience
more common than the latter. Gladys Leonard, one of the most
gifted and highly respected of all mediums, tells us that while
present at the death of her brother-in-law she saw the form of a
girl aged about 18 and dressed in the clothes of some 50 years
ago 'bending over the body in a tender, expectant manner'. Her
brother-in-law's breathing stopped easily and finally, with 'no gasp
or sign of the slightest discomfort; simply withdrawal'. Afterwards,
relatives told her that the description of the young girl fitted that
of the dead man's sister, who had died more than 50 years previously at the age of 18 (Leonard 1937). Natalie Kalmus, known for
her work on colour cinematography, reported that her dying sister,
who was not drugged in any way, lifted herself almost into a sitting
position and spoke of the presence of many unseen visitors –
'There are so many of them ...Fred ... and Ruth ... what's she
doing here? Oh, I know ... so many of them ... I'm going up.' The
reference to Ruth was particularly moving for Natalie Kalmus, as
Ruth was a cousin who had died suddenly the week before, and
whose death was unknown to the dying woman (see Smith 1962).

On other occasions the dying tell of seeing visions of a
beautiful countryside, often peopled with friends and relatives
apparently awaiting them. Whether of places or of people,
deathbed visions typically prompt great joy, enabling the dying

person to pass eagerly out of this life. It is easy to explain away such visions as hallucinations brought on by confusions in the dying brain, but easy explanations are not always the right explanations. As with NDEs, the dying-brain argument fails to account for the coherent and meaningful nature of the visions, or for those cases in which the vision is of someone whose death is unknown to the dying person. It also fails to account for those occasions when the people at the bedside also claim to see the visitors, or for the fact that, as in the case of my mother, the visitors are sometimes first seen some months before death and when the mind of the dying person is mentally alert and free from any medication. In all cases it would be unwise to assume that simply because some-one is nearing the end of their life they are unable to give reliable accounts of their experiences. The dying-brain argument also takes no account of the fact that the visions typically bring great reassurance and joy to the dying. There are very few recorded cases in which the dying express fear that the 'visitors' will take them away against their will, and it seems likely that this fear has more to do with a terror of dying than with anything frightening about the visitors themselves.

Those who appear in deathbed visions are sometimes referred to as 'helpers', and it is said that they accompany the dying person on the journey to the afterlife and help him or her accept death. Fear of death is one of the most primal and understandable of all our fears. Death not only arouses a fear of annihilation but a fear of the unknown, and our survival instinct fights hard against it. Yet death is a natural part of life. Each moment of time lives briefly then dies. Each cell in the body lives its short span and then dies. If we believe in a Creator we accept that this is the way things are meant to be. The poet Dylan Thomas wrote that his dying father should 'Go not gently into that good night, but rage rage against the dying of the light', but an even greater poet – John Keats – wrote that 'Oft have I been in love with easeful death, to cease upon a midnight with no pain'. Very different sentiments but, whatever the sentiment, death remains inescapable, and it makes sense to suppose the 'helpers' may be there to remind and reassure the dying of the fact.

Nurses who work with the dying tell me that deathbed visions are very common, something born out by the findings of Dr Karlis Osis (Osis and Haraldsson 1986). Osis contacted 5,000 American physicians and 5,000 nurses to ask if they had had dying patients who reported visions. Some 640 replied with accounts of 1,318 dying patients who had claimed visions of people and 884 who had claimed visions of beautiful environments such as heavenly cities or gardens. The great majority of these cases did not appear to be ordinary hallucinations as they were coherent and meaningful, unlike the rambling, disjointed visions reported by those patients with medical conditions predisposing them to hallucinate. Furthermore, the hallucinations of the latter were concerned primarily with earthly concerns and memories. Of the patients with non-hallucinatory visions, 753 were also reported by medical personnel to have shown mood elevation shortly before death, and overall, the findings suggested to Dr Osis that dying patients:

- report seeing apparitions more often when fully conscious than when consciousness is impaired;

- report visions much more frequently than do patients not near death;

- report visions usually of close deceased relatives;

- frequently show exaltation before death.

In addition, age, sex and personality of the dying did not influence frequency of visions, nor did drugs appear responsible for their occurrence. Of those dying within 10 minutes of seeing visions, 76 per cent announced the visitors had come to take them away, while fewer than 44 per cent of those dying over an hour later made the same claim.

Dr Osis' overall conclusion was that these results 'are supportive of the afterlife hypothesis', and warrant further research. Accordingly, together with Professor Erlendur Haraldsson, he contacted a further 5,000 doctors and nurses in the USA – 1,004 of whom responded – and 704 medical personnel in India, almost all of whom replied. The two samples were asked to report on hallucinations of people or places, both by the terminally ill and by patients who had been close to death but who subsequently recovered. The samples were also asked to report on any evidence of mood elevation in their patients. Results were consistent with those of Osis' first study. Approximately half of those responding reported cases of hallucinations in the terminally ill, and follow-up interviews by the researchers established that in most instances these hallucinations related to an apparent post-mortem existence. Only in very rare cases did the patients doubt the visions that they had seen. Some 80 per cent of these visions were either of deceased relatives (in the USA) or religious figures (in India). In 65 per cent of cases the dying considered these 'visitors' were there to take them away. Half the visions lasted up to 5 minutes, 17 per cent from 6 to 15 minutes, and 17 per cent for an hour or more. Death followed more quickly after visions relating to the afterlife than after visions relating to worldly concerns.

In the USA the number of men and women seeing visions was virtually equal, but in India twice as many men as women were involved, perhaps because more men than women were at that time admitted to hospital. In both the USA and India, those with a college education were *more* likely to experience visions than those without, although those with religious affiliations experienced visions only slightly more frequently than those with no affiliations.

As with Osis' previous study, hallucinatory drugs such as morphine did not influence the incidence or the characteristics of visions, while brain damage caused by disease, injury or poisoning was generally related to a *decrease* in their incidence. Factors such as stress, expectations of death or of recovery, previous history of hallucinogenic experiences, or a longing to see a living relative or friend before death also appeared to play no part in the occurrence of visions.

The authors concluded that in both the USA and in India, 80 per cent of deathbed visions are of other-worldly figures (deceased relatives or religious beings), whereas only a small minority of hallucinations in the general population are of these subjects. In most cases patients reported that the purpose of the 'visitors' was to take them to the next world, irrespective of their own wishes. Nearly all the American patients and two-thirds of the Indian patients were ready to go after seeing the visions, and most patients were left with positive emotions such as serenity and peace. Those few who expressed negative emotions were predominantly patients whose visions were concerned with this world, and such patients rarely experienced religious feelings.

Apart from the greater incidence of deceased relatives in the deathbed visions reported in America and the greater incidence of religious figures reported in India there were no significant cultural differences between the visions in the two countries. As in the work referred to earlier by Osis and Haraldsson on NDEs, a 'core experience' was identifiable in both cultures that was 'supportive of the post-mortem survival hypothesis'. Also significant was the finding that the afterlife environment experienced by Christians was of a benign and pleasant nature, with an almost total absence of visions of devils or hell, while the experiences of Hindus (as in NDEs) contained no reference to reincarnation or to the various Vedic levels of heaven and the dissolution of self in Brahman, and only vague suggestions emerged of the operation of any law of karma.

The results of this work by Osis and Haraldsson are of major importance to our understanding of dying and of the afterlife. There is a possibility of course that the information collected by them might have been inaccurate, or that their preconceptions might have influenced results (although both researchers began their work with somewhat sceptical attitudes), or that there might have been errors in reporting by medical personnel. There is also the possibility that, in spite of evidence to the contrary, the terminally ill patients may have been influenced by what they had read. However, the similarities between the results obtained in Osis' first study and in the larger study, and between the American and Indian results, support the view that the researchers are correct in concluding they are supportive of the afterlife hypothesis.

The life review

Before proceeding to discuss what may happen after death has taken place, something must be said about the so-called 'life review', mentioned earlier. Most of us will have heard the claim that the drowning man sees the whole of his life flash before him. A colleague and close friend of mine who narrowly escaped drowning described the experience to me as happening 'simultaneously and panoramically', and similar accounts are given in some NDE reports and in many post-mortem communications through mediums. One of the communicators mentioned by Mateu (1999) reports that 'Every feeling, thought, and experience I had ever felt in my entire life, I saw in one fell swoop … a flash of light … an awesome display of the love I had shared and the people I had touched … and the pain I had caused.' How can one's whole life flash before one in the brief interval between life and death (or as some communicators tell us soon after death)? The answer may be that for a few brief moments the mind is outside time, and experiencing a bird's-eye view of all that has led up to that moment. The life review thus becomes a single experience, as if we all have a complete record of our lives within us, and become aware of it on the threshold or a little after death.

Heath and Klimo (2006) point out that the life review is the 'most consistent and universal stage described, regardless of the culture or era ... Ancient Egyptian writings and the Islamic Book of the Dead' and modern communications through mediums 'all state that souls must go through this' before they are ready to move on to higher levels in the afterlife.

But what is the point of this life review? As we shall see in Chapter 9, it appears to be repeated at greater length later in the afterlife with the purpose of helping the individual reflect upon the lessons of his or her time on earth. The shortened version that can happen in an NDE, or shortly after death, may help demonstrate that we are not merely *influenced by* past events, we carry these events with us. Normally we think of our 'self' as what we are in the present, but the life review seems to remind us that although the body displays the badge of our years, our essential self is outside time, with each experience an equally valid part of the whole. At each moment we are our childhood, our adolescence and our adulthood. The poet T S Eliot expresses this concept in *Death by Water* when he tells us that the drowned sailor passes 'again the ages of his age and youth'.

Descriptions of the life review indicate that it is not like *thinking about* what has gone before, it is as if one is back within the experiences and emotions concerned, like entering a picture book instead of just turning the pages. Critics may dismiss such descriptions as fabrications, but critics who have not had the experience themselves would be unwise to try to impose their interpretation of it on those who have.

Chapter Three

·

WHAT HAPPENS NEXT?

Witnessing the moment of passing

What indeed does happen after the last moments on Earth, during which many of the dying reportedly see visions of deceased family and friends and/or of heavenly scenery, and depart this life calmly and peacefully and on occasions even eagerly? Is the promise held out by these visions (and by those experienced in NDEs) realized?

Let's start with what is sometimes seen to leave the body at physical death. In Chapter 2 reference was made to a report by Dr Rentz of a bereaved husband who for some five hours apparently saw a 'nude white body' which he assumed was the 'astral body' floating in a horizontal position above his dying wife connected to her physical body by a 'cord' from the forehead. At the moment of death he witnessed the 'cord' break, and the 'astral body' vanish. This nude body does indeed resemble the non-material 'astral body' that in Eastern and some Western esoteric traditions is said to provide the link between the soul and the physical body, and to leave the latter at death.

References to the 'cord' connecting the astral to the physical body also sometimes occur in the literature on OBEs, with the suggestion that when the cord breaks, death takes place and return to the body is impossible (*see* Crookall 1964, Muldoon and Carrington 1987). OBEs, although they can occur to those in good health, are similar to NDEs in that the consciousness is claimed to leave the physical body for a short time, either spontaneously or as a result of certain visualization and meditative practices. The biblical reference to the time when the 'the silver cord be loosed or the golden bowl be broken' (Ecclesiastes 12:6) is sometimes taken to describe the breaking of the cord at the moment of death.

Another account of witnessing the astral body leaving the physical body at death is by the Reverend Archie Matson, a minister of religion with a particular interest in mystical experiences. The mother of a teacher friend of his, named Mary, was dying of cancer, and near the end Mary experienced a 'strong feeling that would not be denied' that she should look at her mother, whose face was serene. 'Floating from and above her toward the ceiling' Mary saw 'a bright, golden, shapeless mist – heavier in some places than in others'. The doctor sitting with her confirmed he saw the same thing, and that it was not unusual (rather unconvincingly he thought it to be 'gas leaving the body'). She was then told it was time to leave the room as death was imminent (Matson 1975). Crookall, whose work we first met in connection with NDEs, collected many such accounts and communications received through mediums, and concluded that the consciousness leaves the physical body:

> ... at first in an ill-defined, smoke-like mass [that] gradually takes the form of the physical body. If the person is recumbent, the exteriorized double usually lies *horizontally* above the corpse ... from a few inches to a few feet only... Then the double ... stands erect, often looking down on the corpse.
>
> (Crookall 1974)

If Crookall is correct, we can assume that the bereaved husband mentioned by Dr Rentz apparently saw the 'double' of his wife shortly after the exteriorization had taken place, when the 'shapeless mist' had already formed itself into an exact copy of her physical body, while Mary left the room before the cloud assumed the shape of her dying mother.

Dr Crookall's theory that the 'shapeless cloud' precedes the formation of a duplicate body is supported by the experience which he quotes of Dr R Hout, an American physician, who knew nothing of the cord and had never read descriptions of the soul leaving the body. Dr Hout relates that while at the deathbed of his aunt his attention was called 'in some inexplicable way to something above the physical body'. What he saw, about two feet above the bed, was a:

> ... vague outline of a hazy, fog-like substance ... suspended motionless ... Then I was astonished to see definite outlines present themselves, and soon I saw this *fog-like substance was assuming a human form* ... [that] resembled the physical body of my aunt.

The form was 'quiet, serene and in repose', even though the physical body was writhing unconsciously. The features were plainly seen and very similar to the physical face save for a:

> ... glow of peace and vigour ... instead of age and pain. The eyes were closed as though in tranquil sleep, and a luminosity seemed to radiate from the spirit body ... a silver-like substance ... was streaming from the head of the physical body to the head of the spirit double ... at the base of the skull. [The cord seemed] alive with vibrant energy ... I could see pulsations of light stream along the course of it, ... from the physical body to the spirit double ... With each pulsation the spirit-body became more alive and denser, whereas the physical body

became quieter and more nearly lifeless. [This process contin-
ued until the] silver cord snapped and the spirit-body was free.

At this point the eyes of the spirit-body opened, a smile of farewell
followed, and the spirit-body vanished. During this process Dr
Hout was also aware that his aunt's deceased husband and son
were standing beside the bed (like the 'helpers' we met in the
previous chapter).

A similar account is given by E W Oaten, who was watching at
the bedside of Daisy, a dying friend (Oaten 1938). Oaten reports a
stream of 'faint, smoke-like vapour' some few feet above Daisy's
body that grew larger until it gradually assumed 'the form of a
roughly-moulded dummy of the human form to which it was
attached by an umbilical cord through which a flow of energy was
visible'. Gradually the form became 'an exact duplicate of Daisy's
body [and began] to heave and rock, like a balloon tearing at
its moorings'. The silver cord grew thinner and thinner until it
snapped and the floating form assumed an upright attitude.
Daisy then turned and smiled at Oaten, while from 'near the
ceiling there came ... two white-robed figures, a man and a woman
... wrapping their robes about her they floated away.'

One of the questions that comes immediately to mind is why
experiences like this are not more common. Normally nothing
unusual is seen by those gathered at the bedside of the dying. One
possible answer is that a degree of clairvoyance (the ability to see
by senses other than the physical) is necessary in the onlookers. A
strong emotional bond with the dying person may also be helpful.
Another possibility is that the initiative may come from the dying,
a few of whom may have the ability (consciously or unconsciously)
to involve onlookers in their deathbed experiences. Modern drugs
that render the dying unconscious may interfere with this ability,
which may explain why fewer deathbed visions are currently
reported than hitherto. Possibly this is the same ability responsible
for sightings of individuals who are having OBEs.

I have personal experience of such sightings, having seen fellow psychologist and close friend and colleague Ingrid Slack while she was out of her body. On the occasion concerned I was awake, in good health and not on drugs of any kind, and saw her so clearly and objectively that initially I was convinced she was physically present. I actually spoke to her before she gradually became increasingly transparent and disappeared. We had made no pact to experiment with OBEs and the occurrence was totally unexpected (I give a full account of it in *Is There an Afterlife?*). Such experiences make it much less easy for me to dismiss the idea of a non-material astral body, a duplicate of the physical, that can existindependently of the latter and may leave it along with the soul at the moment of death.

Has the 'astral body' been sighted in the living?

There are in fact numerous similar claims in the literature, of living individuals seen when apparently out of their physical bodies. Sightings include a number of the Christian saints, and the Roman Catholic Church – notoriously strict in its official recognition of miracles – accepts the reality of several of them, such as that of St Anthony of Padua who, while preaching in the church of St Pierre at Limoges on Holy Thursday in 1226, remembered he was due to read the lesson in a monastery on the other side of town. Reportedly he drew his hood over his head and knelt down in prayer while his congregation waited patiently in silence. Simultaneously he was seen by the monks at the monastery to step from a stall in the monastery chapel, read the appointed lesson, and immediately disappear.

Similar accounts exist for St Severus of Ravenna, St Ambrose of Rome and St Clement of Rome. A particularly well-attested case is that of St Alphonse of Liguori who, when confined to his cell in 1774 due to a dispute over doctrinal matters with his brethren, fell into a trance for some five days, after which he gave the news that he had been at the death-bed of Pope Clement XIV, four days journey away. Not only was the news of the pontiff's death unexpected, those at the deathbed subsequently confirmed that St Alphonse had been present with them at the time.

We have no way of checking the accuracy of these early accounts, and it is easy to dismiss them as attempts to enhance the status of the saints concerned, but this would do less than justice to the scrupulous care (equal in many ways to that of modern psychical researchers) with which the Roman Catholic Church investigates supposed miracles before accepting their authenticity.

However, well-attested cases are not confined to the Catholic Church and its saints. One of the best-known is that of Vincent Turvey, who had frequent OBEs in the course of which he was often seen by observers who gave signed testimony to this effect. In one example the witness was writing in his room when he tells us he:

> ... became conscious of someone being present and turned round expecting to find my wife standing in the doorway. You can imagine my surprise to see a shadowy ethereal form, which I was able to recognize as [Turvey]. I waited for some sign or impression, but got neither; but watched the form disappear ... in the darkness of the hall.

Another witness informs Turvey that he is:

> ... quite willing to testify to the fact that I have seen 'you' when your body was hundreds of miles away from me. I am not a clairvoyant and was not asleep at the time ... I [once] distinctly saw you three-quarter length floating in the air ... I called out in fear and you immediately vanished.

Another witness claimed to see Turvey while:

> I was at a séance at least two miles from your house ... I saw
> distinctly what, for want of better words, I must call 'you in the
> spirit body'. I felt it was so *real* that I must get up and place a
> chair for you.

Not only were these and other testimonies to Turvey's appearance
signed by the witnesses, the original copies of them were read and
checked by a panel of named individuals of apparent social and
academic standing who certified that:

> In our opinion the letters [concerned] are absolutely genuine
> correspondence given or sent to Mr Turvey as evidence for
> some super-normal faculty possessed by him ... We think Mr
> Turvey's state of health [which for many years was so poor it
> brought him close to death on several occasions] makes it
> impossible for him to have used any method of espionage, and
> we do not think he is morally capable of attempting so to do.

Turvey's book detailing his experiences has a lengthy preface by
W T Stead, one of the most noted psychical researchers of the
early 20th century, who knew Turvey well and stresses that 'I
believe Mr Turvey is a man of truth, that his testimony is trust-
worthy evidence ... and that the witnesses' letters which are held
for the scrutiny of inquirers are the genuine epistles of credible
witnesses' (Turvey 1969). Stead was not in the habit of endorsing
the work of unreliable authors.

Let me give just one more example of sightings of the so-called
astral body of the living, since the existence of these cases makes it
easier to accept such a body may leave the physical at death. Harold
Sherman, who became famous for the successful long-distance
telepathy experiments he carried out with explorer Sir Hubert
Wilkins while the latter was north of the Arctic Circle and
Sherman was in New York (Wilkins and Sherman 1971) tells of a

close friend of his, Harry Loose, a retired police officer with strong psychic abilities, who left a verbal message for him with William Cousins, the desk clerk at Sherman's apartment block. The message, which Cousins wrote down as it was given to him, was to the effect that Loose was expecting a visit from Sherman and his wife the following Sunday. However, when Sherman read the message on his return home and telephoned Loose, the latter insisted he had not left his house, some 20 miles away, all day. Upon inquiry Cousins, who had never met Harry Loose, described him exactly, down to the shabby casual clothes he was wearing. Sherman then arranged for Loose to visit the apartment block when the unsuspecting Cousins was on duty, with Sherman observing unseen from just outside the reception area. Loose wore the same casual clothes as previously except for a lighter-coloured shirt, and on arrival at the reception desk he was recognized and greeted by name by Cousins, who in the ensuing conversation with Loose and Sherman even volunteered the information that Loose was not wearing the same shirt as previously.

When publishing the case Sherman included signed statements from four members of the Loose family to the effect that Harry Loose could not have driven the round trip of 40 miles to Sherman's apartment block on the day Cousins first claimed to have seen him, and a lengthy signed statement from Cousins, who was now told the full story, confirming each of the details of his two meetings with Loose. In the course of his statement Cousins described the experience as 'the most thrilling happening of my life'.

Taken together, these statements by people of good character would be quite sufficient to carry conviction in a court of law. In addition, Harry Loose had nothing to gain from mounting an elaborate hoax. Suffering from a serious heart condition he wanted no publicity over the incident, preferring to keep his psychic abilities confidential both for his own sake and for that of his family. He insisted Sherman could only publish the case after his death, which occurred almost to the day two years after the incident (Sherman 1972).

There is a long tradition in the more esoteric Western traditions that the physical body is linked to three non-physical bodies, namely an energy body, an astral body and a soul body. The energy body is said to sustain the physical body during life and to be discarded some three days after death, leaving the astral and the soul body to continue the journey into the afterlife. In some ways this seems in keeping with the Christian teaching on the resurrection of 'the body'. For centuries the assumption was that this meant the actual *physical* body, as Christ appeared after death in his physical form to his disciples, but the teaching is now more generally thought to apply to the soul body, which after death is said to resemble the physical body, at least until it becomes more spiritually advanced and the astral body is in turn discarded.

Life without a physical body

We shall have more to say about this in subsequent chapters, but what might existence be like without the actual physical body? In this world our experiences come to us through our physical senses, and many people therefore find it hard to conceive of a non-physical existence. However, our experiences in dreams give us some idea. Our dream body still feels to us to be a 'real' body, apparently capable of seeing, hearing, touching, experiencing emotions and even eating and drinking. We 'walk', we 'run', we 'speak' – we do pretty well everything with our dream bodies that we do with our physical bodies. In fact, to all intents and purposes we feel as fully embodied in dreams as we do when awake.

A similar feeling of being in command of all the physical senses is reported by some of those who have experienced an NDE or an OBE. True, there are accounts of some in the NDE or OBE state or who have no consciousness of a body, but most individuals are aware of themselves as embodied – even as a body that can be recognized by others as if physically present as we saw in the above examples. In cases where the physical body is in pain the pain is not replicated in the projected body, although the latter reportedly feels emotions such as peace and occasionally fear. Sometimes there are reports of 'seeing' details in the physical surroundings and of 'hearing' what physical beings are saying, and overall it seems that the projected body (which presumably contains both astral and soul bodies which in turn include mind and consciousness) is experienced in similar ways to the physical. In some NDEs there is even reference to a clarity of mind and senses greater than that experienced when in the physical.

Commenting upon the important distinction between the inner world of perceptions and feelings and the sensory awareness of the outer world registered through the physical body, Professor Hyslop – former professor of logic and ethics at Columbia University and a leading early psychical researcher – puts it that:

> In normal life the internal activities of the mind have their own existence and meaning apart from sensory experience, though condemned to work ... [with this experience]. There is in them [i.e. in the internal activities] the beginning of a spiritual life, the foreshadowing of an independent existence ... and death only liberates the inner life from the shackles of sensation and enhances its creative power.
>
> (Hyslop 1918)

The next question is of what substance is the projected body, free from what Hyslop calls 'the shackles of [bodily] sensation', composed? The fact that it can sometimes be seen by the living suggests it is quasi-physical, unless we take the view it is seen by a form of 'clairvoyant' vision rather than physical vision. The second possibility is that it is a thought body. We all carry in our minds an image of how we look, and it may be that this image can take on a quasi-objective existence, visible in certain circumstances by witnesses. These two possibilities will be returned to when we discuss the hypothetical nature of the next world in later chapters.

Science has no way of detecting astral or soul bodies, but photographs supposedly of apparitions – some rather more convincing than others – taken at séances and elsewhere do exist (see e.g. Chéroux et al 2005 and Willin 2007). There is in addition some informal speculation that the meridians (the supposed energy channels throughout the body needled during acupuncture) may be evidence of a non-physical body of some kind, since although they are not conclusively detectable scientifically there is no doubt they play some role in physical health and healing. The chakras – supposedly centres of this non-physical energy – situated successively from the perineum upwards to the crown and an integral part of Hindu philosophies such as Yoga may also, if they exist, be related to a non-physical body.

Sceptics have an understandable dislike of any mention of subtle energies and non-physical bodies since the terms are often used so loosely, yet experience over many centuries by Eastern holy men and physicians suggests that they are a reality. Incidentally, if there were no sightings of an apparently non-physical body leaving at the moment of death and no reports of NDEs or of other-worldly visions by the dying, then there is little doubt that sceptics would claim this as support for their argument that death is the end of everything.

'Crossing over' and books of the dead

Space allows us only a brief look at the many descriptions by different spiritual traditions of the actual boundary between life and death (*see* e.g. Neiman and Goldman 1994 for a summary) in order to see if they possess any similarities with the modern accounts we have been discussing. Most traditions do indeed refer to a period of darkness on leaving the body, similar to NDE references to a dark 'tunnel'. They also describe a barrier or threshold encountered after death and to a 'guardian' of the threshold whose task may be to send back those whose time, as in NDEs, has not yet come. In the ancient Greek traditions this barrier was linked to a symbolic river, the River Styx, complete with a boatman, Charon, who ferried the dead across to the other shore. For the Greeks this crossing was considered hazardous, and the dead were traditionally buried with a coin to pay Charon for a safe crossing, as it was feared that if they fell into the Styx it would sweep them down to Tartares, the lowest level of the underworld. There are similarities between Charon and the frequent references in modern reports to the presence of 'helpers' who assist the dying, while the primitive idea of a 'coin' and the possible descent into Tartares may have some symbolic similarities with the contemporary references to purgatory to which we turn in the next chapter.

The ancient Egyptians actually buried the dead with elaborate written instructions on how to cross this symbolic boundary (or boundaries) between the worlds. The oldest of the so-called Pyramid Texts (intended initially only for kings), dating from between 2340 and 2175 BCE and among the earliest surviving writings in human history, all reflect the enduring Egyptian belief in the immortality of the soul and in resurrection after death (*see* Budge 1972 and Grof 1994). One of the persistent ideological themes in these Texts is an emphasis upon light in the form of the sun god Ra, and on the wish to join him after death in the splendid solar boat in which he travelled across the skies. The knowledge of certain magic formulae and words of power were needed to pass safely through the various boundaries, each of them guarded by fearsome beings who seem like forerunners of the frightening visions reported by those with negative NDE experiences such as Howard Storm (Storm 2000).

A second persistent theme in these ancient Egyptian Books of the Dead is that of judgement. Those faithful to Osiris, the ruler of the afterlife, and who have lived a good life, are destined to be with him in Sekhet Hetepet, the 'Happy Fields', and to join him in worship and feasting and in tending the beautiful plants and trees. The wicked and the enemies of Ra and Osiris are destined for punishments, some of which are detailed in the texts.

The Egyptian conviction of survival of death was based not only upon belief in Osiris. In the sacred temple mysteries (initiatory rites) of Isis and Osiris the neophytes (fledgling priests) actually went through a secret initiation in which they confronted death and experienced what appears to have been an out-of-the-body experience that took from them any fear of death and assured them of their own immortality. The later Greek mysteries of Isis and of Demeter (the goddess of fertility) used similar rites, again removing all fear of death. The details of the full initiations were guarded by oaths of secrecy, so rigidly kept that we still do not know the full details, but hints are given by Apuleius (first century CE) in his text *The Golden Ass*, a satire upon the vices and follies of men that concludes with his own initiation into the mysteries of Isis.

A book of the dead that has become particularly well known in the West since its translation into English in 1927 by the Oxford University anthropologist W Y Evans-Wentz and the Tibetan Lama Dawa-Samdup, is the Tibetan Bardo Thodol, which catalogues in graphic detail the experiences of the deceased in the immediate afterlife. This extraordinary book raises so many issues associated with Tibetan Buddhist beliefs in reincarnation/rebirth that it is more appropriate to leave it for discussion until Chapter 8, but books of the dead were also a feature of Western medieval Christianity. The best known is the *Ars Bene Moriendi* (the *Art of Dying Well*), which insists that, when approaching death, the mind should 'reject all transitory things as if they are poison' and should turn instead towards prayer and the surrender of the self to God. It teaches that the prayer 'Lord thou hast broken my bonds; I will sacrifice to thee the sacrifice of praise' is particularly powerful in obtaining remittance of sins if said in truth and sincerity, and that one's last words should be 'Into they hands I commit my spirit' (*see* Shinners 2007).

The *Ars Bene Moriendi* was intended as a potent reminder of the inevitability of death, and like other books of the dead was designed to be studied by the living as well as read to the dying. It taught that life is in part a preparation for death, and that the quality of this preparation helps determine how well one manages the transition to the next world. It advises that prayers to Christ, to the Holy Virgin and to the archangel Michael should be read to the dying, and describes the various challenges encountered as the consciousness slips from one world to the next. Described as 'attacks of Satan', these challenges were seen as the devil's attempts to divert the soul from its path to heaven. They included a weakening of faith, despair as to the fate of one's soul, pride in one's earthly achievements, impatience at one's physical sufferings, attachments to one's material possessions, concentration upon one's sins instead of upon prayers for forgiveness, and grievances over perceived worldly injustices.

The importance of one's state of mind while dying will be discussed more fully in the next chapter, but the *Ars Bene Moriendi* also sought to give the dying a foretaste of the bliss of heaven and reminders of the enduring love and mercy of Christ and of the help always available to those who truly repented their misdoings and sincerely call upon Christ for help.

The impression given by the *Ars Bene Moriendi* is that the instructions it contains are relevant not only in the hours before dying but also as one passes into the afterlife. It is made clear that the dying mind that is devout and humble and turned in love and devotion to God the Father, to Christ, to the Holy Spirit and to the Holy Virgin and the archangel Michael will remain in the same state after death, and receive through grace a peaceful and blessed passage in the next world. Like so much medieval sacred literature it also brings home to the reader the impermanent nature of earthly goals and the ever-present threat of death, facts that were also emphasized by other means such as symbols like the four horsemen of the apocalypse (war, famine, plague and death), and the human skull that a scholar would keep on his desk as a *memento mori*.

Warnings such as 'Thus will ye be, and as you are so were we' were often written beside images of skeletons, and the 'Dance of Death' (*Danse Macabre*), a series of pictures showing the living dancing with skeletons or corpses that led them towards the tomb, further emphasized the message. All – from kings and nobles to the humblest servant – would in due course become part of this eerie dance, and in consequence the mind should be continually turning towards God and the afterlife. To the modern Western mind this may all seem very over-exaggerated, but perhaps we have gone rather too far in the opposite direction and over-insulated ourselves from the fact of our ever present mortality.

Last words

It is appropriate to conclude this chapter with some of the reported last words of well-known men and women that suggest they were witnessing something rare and beautiful. Thomas Edison, responsible for the fact we have electricity in our homes, said 'It is very beautiful over there'. Frederic Chopin, the finest of all those who wrote for the piano, said 'Now I am the source of all blessedness', while another great composer, Gustav Mahler, called out 'Mozart!' (one of his musical inspirations). Beethoven, whose deafness prevented him from hearing his own music, said 'In heaven I shall hear'. That most wonderful and visionary of painters, William Turner, said 'The sun is God'. Also on the subject of light the great German writer and mystic Johann von Goethe announced 'More light!', and George Selwyn the Bishop of Lichfield insisted 'It is all light!'. The great French writer Jean

Jacques Rousseau called out 'See the sun ... There is God Himself who is opening His arms and inviting me to taste at last that eternal and unchanging joy that I have so long desired'. Elizabeth Barrett Browning, one of the most profoundly moving of all women poets and the wife of Robert Browning, uttered the single word 'Beautiful'. The 19th-century French monarch Louis XVII said 'The music is so beautiful ... listen listen, in the midst of all those voices I hear my mother' (the tragic queen Marie Antoinette). The great dancer Vaslav Nijinsky was another who seemed to see his deceased mother, calling out to her with his last breath, while Antonio Canova, sculptor of sublime masterpieces, repeated several times 'Pure and loving spirit ...'.

Chapter Four

·

SUDDEN DEATH AND STATES OF MIND

Prayers for deliverance from sudden death

Staying a little longer with the medieval theme introduced towards the end of the last chapter, there is an old prayer that asks God for deliverance from various evils and dangers including '... and sudden death'. Why sudden death? Is a sudden death worse than a more gradual one? We can get a hint of the answer by imagining we are abruptly woken from a very deep sleep to find ourselves outside our bodies and desperately but fruitlessly trying to attract the attention of others to our plight, and then finding ourselves transported to a strange and foggy environment where we attempt, with mounting alarm, to make out what has happened. Such a scenario gives us some idea of what sudden death might be like. Disorientated and thrust from a familiar world into a strange place of darkness and loneliness our panic would be like that of a small child lost in the deserted mist-bound streets of an unknown city.

The experience of sudden death

What evidence is there that sudden and totally unexpected death may be something like that? Firstly, there is the confusion reported by a few individuals such as Daniel Gélin (Chapter 2) during negative NDE experiences when they find themselves outside their bodies and trying desperately to make contact with medical staff. Secondly, there is the extensive information from mediums who report having received communications from those who have died suddenly.

Many examples of these communications were collected by Air Chief Marshal Lord Dowding, who in his role as Head of British Fighter Command during the early months of the Second World War was in charge of the British fighter pilots who repulsed German aircraft and did much to avert a threatened invasion of Britain. The Battle of Britain, as it came to be called, involved constant aerial battles from 10 July 1940 to 31 October 1940 that only ended with the defeat of the German invasion plans. Regarded as one of the most important engagements of the Second World War, the Battle of Britain involved the death of 544 British airmen (one in four of all those who flew) and the wounding of many more. Lord Dowding, a deeply humane and sensitive man, felt very keenly that it was he who, albeit in the unavoidable line of duty, had sent these young men to their deaths.

Deeply troubled, he began to explore the evidence for life after death, and wrote a bestselling account of his findings under the title *Many Mansions*. After the appearance of *Many Mansions* he accepted an invitation to sit regularly with a group led by a non-professional medium known as 'L L' that reported receiving regular communications from the deceased. During his first sitting a communicator quoted to him, through 'L L', the final sentence of the book on which he was currently working, namely 'Now therefore, as I lay down my sword, I take up my pen'. This, to Dowding, was very impressive, as the book was still only in manuscript form and nobody in the group knew of its existence let alone its final line.

From then on, Dowding took the communications seriously, particularly as some of them appeared to be from young servicemen killed in the war (Dowding 1945 and 1951). Many of these communications contained detailed accounts of sudden and unexpected death, and it was clear that often those involved remained unaware they were dead. Dowding saw it as his duty to acquaint them with the facts of death and to help them move on to the next stage of their lives. Here is an example, in abbreviated form, of a communicator (through the entranced medium L L) who describes himself as a squadron leader, present with the rest of his aircrew. He is puzzled as to where he now is, and when told he is in London he expresses great surprise.

SQUADRON LEADER: *But how did we get here? We were shot down over the Ruhr* [Germany].

DOWDING: *You have been brought here so that we can help you.*

SQUADRON LEADER: *But who are you?* [Dowding reveals his identity, and his name is immediately recognized by the Squadron Leader]. *How can you help us?* [Dowding holds out a hand and the entranced medium indicates that the Squadron Leader realizes he can see the hand but cannot grasp it].

SQUADRON LEADER: *Look here Sir, are you trying to tell us that we are – that this is death?*

DOWDING: *Yes.*

SQUADRON LEADER: *But how can we be dead? We are just as we were before.*

DOWDING: *Now you can see what a ridiculous little barrier death is.*

THE TAIL GUNNER: [joining the conversation] *I remember a Hun fighter coming up behind ... Then I remember no more until we were in the road outside.*

Subsequently, Dowding is told by one of the medium's regular communicators that the plane in which the crew was flying had blown up when hit by enemy gunfire, and that all the crew were killed. By dying together and being continually aware of each other's company they escaped some of the disorientation reportedly felt when individuals die suddenly when alone, but still failed to recognize what had happened to them. (The reader may wonder how the airmen had occupied themselves during the period between their crash and their meeting with Dowding, and the probable answer is that time as we know it had not passed for them, a phenomenon discussed in Chapter 9).

Numerous accounts similar to the above were received by mediums during and after both the First and the Second World War. One of the best-known examples after the former war was that communicated through Wellesley Tudor Pole and published under the title of *Private Dowding* (no relation to Lord Dowding). Killed while in the front-line trenches, Private Dowding describes his experiences as follows (Tudor Pole, W. 1984).

One moment I was alive ... looking over a trench parapet, unalarmed, normal. Five seconds later I was standing outside my body, helping two of my pals carry my body down the trench towards a dressing station. They thought I was senseless but alive. I did not know whether I had jumped out of my body through shell shock, temporarily or for ever. You see what a small thing is death, even the violent death of war! I seemed in a dream ... Soon I should wake up and find myself in the traverse waiting to go on guard ... It all happened so simply. Death for me was a simple experience – no horror, no long-drawn suffering, no conflict ... Shock comes later when comprehension dawns: 'Where is my body? Surely I am not dead!' ... When I found that my two pals could carry my body without my help, I dropped behind ... in a curiously humble way. Humble? .... My body was hoisted on to the stretcher. I wondered when I should get back into it again.

... I imagined I was still physically) alive ... I had been struck by a shell splinter ... there was no pain. Then I found that the whole of myself – all, that is, that thinks and sees and feels and knows – was still alive and conscious! ... My body went to the first dressing station, and after examination was taken to a mortuary. I stayed near it all that night, watching, but without thoughts ... I still expected to wake up in my body again ... Then I lost consciousness and slept soundly.

... When I awoke, my body had disappeared! How I hunted and hunted! It began to dawn upon me that something strange had happened ... Then the shock came! It came without warning suddenly ... I was dead! ... I had been killed, killed, killed! ... Now the shock came and it was very real. I tried to think backwards but my memory was numb ...

Dowding tells Tudor Pole subsequently that he had enlisted in the autumn of 1915, spent eight months training in Northumberland, and had left for France with his battalion in July 1916, going to the front almost immediately (probably to the Battle of the Somme, which started in July 1916) and dying there in action a month later. Tudor Pole does not seem to have obtained Dowding's real name and regimental number, and since a large proportion of the army records were destroyed by enemy bombing during the Second World War there is now, in any case, little chance of verifying his existence. So, as with many supposed communications from the deceased, why should we take any of this seriously? Essentially all depends upon our assessment of the reliability of Tudor Pole, a non-professional medium with a reputation for great integrity.

I never met Pole but I knew his granddaughter, a professional woman whose memories of him were of a man of gentle wisdom and of genuine mystic and psychic abilities. Furthermore, he was a close friend and colleague of both Sir George Trevelyan, founder of the well-known Wrekin Trust, and of Rosamond Lehmann, one of the leading female writers of the last century, with both of whom he wrote books on spiritual themes. He was also a friend of Winston Churchill, and together with Churchill founded the 'Silent Minute' to mark the anniversary of the ending of the First World War, which developed into the Armistice Day Remembrance Ceremony observed annually ever since. He was also responsible for setting up the group that preserved the historic Chalice Well at Glastonbury, one of the main objects of veneration at this ancient sacred site.

Whatever we make of the identity of Private Dowding himself, no grounds exist for doubting the honesty and sincerity of Tudor Pole. There is also no doubt that Dowding's account is typical of those given through mediums by many of the soldiers killed suddenly in both the World Wars. There is the same attempt to carry on with normal life and the same fruitless efforts to help or to communicate with the living, the same expectation that one will 'wake up' in the body again, and the same shock and confusion as something of the nature of the changes that have occurred gradually dawn.

Dowding later reports that he eventually lost consciousness and slept, and that after he awoke and found his physical body had disappeared he began 'floating in a mist that muffled sound and blurred the vision'. However, perhaps because during his lifetime he had read a little about the afterlife, he seems to have been spared the confusion and terror that can follow if after sudden death the deceased find themselves in such a shadowy, misty environment reminiscent of the ancient Greek description of Hades and the Jewish descriptions of Sheol, a place of dark shadows where the dead are even said to envy the living (*see* Crookall 1978 for examples).

Jane Sherwood, a respected writer on psychic and spiritual experiences and, like Tudor Pole, a gifted non-professional medium writes in *The Country Beyond* (Sherwood 1969) that 'Scott', one of her communicators who also met sudden death, reports that:

> I think the experience of death must vary considerably because it is governed by the state of mind in which one passes over. Also there is a vast difference between a sudden passing and a quiet and prepared one. The shock of an unnatural death sets the ... being in a mad turmoil ... One finds oneself in a fantastic dream world with no continuity of experience ... the chaos of unconnected states of mind have no proper framework of space and time... Much of this earlier nightmare could [be avoided if one knows how to avail oneself] of the help that [is] freely offered.

As with NDEs, it seems that calling for help – in the case of those with a Christian background to Christ or the saints – results in contact with a beneficent spiritual source that leads to release from these frightening experiences.

Other traditions and sudden death

Similar problems of fear and confusion following sudden death are also stressed in non-Christian traditions such as Buddhism and the shamanic religions of Native America and of Asia. Sudden death is in fact seen as an example of dying in the wrong state of mind, since one has little chance of preparing oneself for what is to come. Tibetan Buddhism in particular stresses that if one is in a state of fear, or of anger or bitterness (as would be likely for those who die in battle), or distracted by material concerns or attachments to worldly goods, the result is a confused and disturbing entry into the next world even if one has lived a blamelessly moral and spiritual life. Unless the mind is tranquil and fully accepting at the moment of death, it is unable to experience the tranquil transition to the next world, essential if one is to remain properly aware of what is happening and to have some control over the immediate afterlife state.

A Tibetan Buddhist monk once put it to me that dying with an unprepared mind inevitably impels one to return for another life-time in the physical world, with all the challenges and potential suffering that such rebirth entails. In other words, one's prepara-tion for the next world must continue right up until one draws the final breath.

We shall return to the possible relevance of these Tibetan teach-ings to our understanding of the afterlife in Chapter 8, but they may help explain why the unpleasant experiences reported as sometimes occurring during NDEs can happen to good individu-als as well as to the less deserving, as the former individuals may be particularly anxious over the welfare of those they leave behind or over worthwhile tasks still unfulfilled. The teachings may also help explain the emphasis by Buddhism upon the mind training that results from the practice of meditation, an emphasis also found in all the great spiritual traditions. Meditation helps the mind to remain focused and aware rather than fragmented and distracted by its own mental chatter, and not only makes us more effective in dealing with the challenges of daily life but in our spiritual development, and it is no surprise that the clear tranquil mind developed by meditation is said to be the ideal state in which to die.

We may prefer to disregard the notion that the state of mind at death influences what happens next, but there is a logic in suppos-ing that what is going on in our minds when we die may have an effect upon the immediate afterlife experience, particularly as the next world (as we shall see in the following chapter) is said to be largely mentally constructed, and that therefore in many ways it is as true in the next world as it is in this, that as we think so we are.

Suicide

People sometimes ask what happens to suicides in the after-life. Anyone who is desperate enough to wish to take their own life deserves sympathy and support rather than censure, but if communications through mediums are anything to go on (we meet an extreme example of just such a communication in Chapter 5) suicide usually makes for a confused and distressing entry into the afterlife.

This can have two obvious causes. Firstly, the suicide may have no belief in an afterlife, and this lack of belief (as with those without belief who die from natural causes) leaves the individual in a disorientated state. He or she wishes to die or expects to die, and therefore cannot accept that death has actually taken place and is not final after all. Consequently they may still believe they are alive in this world, and we are told that this may result in their remaining earthbound (Chapter 5), unable to communicate either with those on earth or with spirit helpers. Secondly, the suicide is likely to have died in the wrong frame of mind. Understandably in an emotional turmoil, and tormented by anxieties and self-rejec-tion, he or she is then thrust unprepared into the afterlife, and open to all the negative experiences mentioned at the beginning of this chapter.

Heath and Klimo (2006) point out that in this confused state the suicide may also be full of regret for his or her actions, and in this troubled condition may remain in the dark mists of Hades (Chapter 6), isolated and beyond help. One of Jane Sherwood's communicators (*see* Sherwood 1964) tells of meeting in the afterlife a friend who had committed suicide and who:

> … was in a kind of stupor, and I was told that he might remain in this state for a long time and that nothing could be done about it … Suicides often show this long-lasting coma … Knowing the agony of loneliness and 'lostness' one can suffer

in this region of looming shadows ... I hailed him and he let me come up but it was hard to make him see or hear me.

It seems that the soul can remain in this state for many years as we reckon time – until in fact it is able to recognize its position and request help. To us such a request may seem easily made, but it is quite another matter when the mind is in a state of painful confusion and so dominated by misconceptions as to what happens after death that it cannot make the readjustments necessary to reach the level of thought of the spirits waiting to help. However, in the end help is eventually found and the process of recovery commences, but Heath and Klimo imply that recovery may involve reincarnating, as the problems that led to suicide may have to be met and successfully overcome while on earth (the pros and cons of the concept of reincarnation are discussed in Chapter 8).

Chapter Five

·

EARTHBOUND SPIRITS

Those who are unwilling to leave

It is appropriate to begin a description of the afterlife with those unfortunate souls who, for a time at least, seem unwilling or unable to leave the confines of the earth. Referred to as 'earthbound spirits', such individuals are said to remain fixated upon material existence and, in most cases, even to be unaware that they have died. Without help from this world or from the next, it is claimed they may remain 'earthbound' for long periods of time, lost and hopeless in a physical world that still seems familiar to them but with which they find it impossible to interact. They may be aware of those they love and may try desperately to contact them but without success, and some mediums and groups of sitters form themselves into what are called 'rescue circles' in an attempt to attract the attention of these spirits and help them understand what has happened to them and how to move on towards the spirit world.

Mediums claim there are a number of reasons why some spirits remain earthbound, for example:

Sudden death

Attention was drawn in Chapter 4 to the unpleasant consequences following sudden unexpected death, and by way of illustration Air Chief Marshal Dowding's work as a member of a rescue circle, with the spirits of young servicemen who were in this unhappy position, was described. Those who die suddenly are particularly prone to remain unaware – especially if they were fit and well at the time of death – that they have died. They remain conscious of familiar physical surroundings and of the fact that they still feel embodied and unchanged. Aimless and uncomprehending they remain attached to the places they know.

Emotional ties

It is said that the intense grief of the bereaved can keep even relatively advanced souls earthbound. Grief is part of the healing process, but ideally it should also be associated as time goes by with feelings of gratitude and thankfulness for the lives of the departed, rather than with a fruitless desire to cling on to them. Moved by the intense grief of this desire the deceased may be unable to move on. We are told that the living typically cling more strongly to the deceased than the other way around because the reality of survival changes the perspectives of the latter. Nevertheless, those in the afterlife can be deeply disturbed by the suffering of the living. Private Dowding, communicating through Wellesley Tudor Pole (Chapter 4), tells of one of his deceased companions who 'grieved together' with his bereaved wife because of her great suffering over his death.

Desire or unfinished business

A third group is said to remain close to earth because there are things the spirits still wish to see accomplished. Communications through mediums have revealed that they may feel their remains have not been buried in consecrated ground, or there are problems over their possessions, their last wills and bequests, or over their business interests which they see being mishandled by the living. They may be disturbed by what is being done with their possessions or with the organizations or institutions they established when on earth, or they may harbour bitter feelings towards those they feel have wronged them. Whether they are aware of their own deaths or not, their concerns are with this world rather than with the next, and they find great difficulty in being 'released' from this world until these concerns have been addressed by the living or until their earth memories begin to fade.

One of the most widely publicized hauntings in history, that experienced by the Fox family in 1848 at Hydesville in the USA (the haunting that led indirectly to the founding of Spiritualism as a religion), was said to be caused by a peddler apparently murdered in the house by a previous occupant and who wished to bring the crime to public attention. A human skeleton was discovered in the walls of the Fox household 56 years later, prompting the formerly sceptical *Boston Journal* to state at the time that this removed from the Fox sisters 'the only shadow of doubt held concerning their sincerity in the discovery of spirit communications'.

Disbelief in an afterlife

A fourth group of earthbound spirits is said to consist of some of those who have no belief in an afterlife and who, until they accept the fact of their own death, remain in a twilight existence in the physical dimension. It is said that these confused souls may fiercely resent the individuals who now occupy 'their' homes and appear to have stolen 'their' property, or who have formed emotional relationships with 'their' loved ones. Sometimes there are attempts to drive away those they resent by causing as much disturbance as possible, some of it deliberately malevolent. Larsen, who claimed to be able to leave her body at will (in an OBE) and visit the spirit world, said after meeting such individuals that they are '... deluded into believing that they still live in the material [world] and [thus] endeavour to carry on life as they always did' (Larsen 1927).

Poltergeist hauntings by earthbound spirits

It is claimed that spirits who remain earthbound (particularly those in the fourth group listed above) may be responsible for what are called *poltergeist* (a German word meaning a 'disturbing spirit') hauntings, that is hauntings that primarily involve the violent disturbance of objects, loud noises and even attempts to frighten the living into abandoning their homes. Such hauntings have been reported for centuries, and both the Roman Catholic and the Anglican churches recognize their existence and empower priests to conduct exorcism services designed to constrain or banish the entity concerned. Mediums also try to make contact in order to help the entity accept the fact of death and move on to higher dimensions. The need for help from this world, rather than from the next, is said to be because earthbound spirits are too close to the heavy material 'atmosphere' of the earth to be reached by spirit beings until they accept the fact they are deceased and begin to move away from this atmosphere.

I have myself investigated poltergeist cases that included apparent attempts to be both unpleasant and even dangerous. In one such case a fire resulting in hundreds of pounds worth of damage, and requiring the attention of the fire brigade, was started in a bathroom where no normal means for causing fires were present. On another occasion an overall hanging on a peg burst spontaneously into flames in full view of the two terrified women owners of the house. Large objects such as a bookcase were sent crashing to the floor downstairs during the night, and bedding was slashed as if by a razor while the house was empty. Despite summoning the police on three occasions, no evidence of human agency was ever discovered, and even replacing all the locks of the house produced no respite. On one occasion a visitor was struck painfully on the back of the head by a bunch of keys thrown from behind while she was descending the stairs.

However, not all poltergeist hauntings by earthbound spirits are ill-intentioned. Some investigators report receiving the impression that the spirit concerned is simply lonely and anxious to attract attention. I investigated a case of this kind, centred on a small engineering workshop and retail shop in Cardiff, that appeared to be associated with a small boy, and I witnessed mischievous examples of physical disturbances even when in the 'haunted' premises on my own, which effectively ruled out any possibility of trickery by the living.

The source of the disturbances, whether a small boy or not (I confirmed with a member of his family that a small boy had in fact been killed in a road accident nearby shortly before the haunting began, and an adult relative of the owners of the premises saw the apparition of a small boy in good light in the workshop on three occasions), manifested a ready intelligence and a desire to be playful, even responding to requests from the living to hit designated objects on the premises with the small stones that 'he' persisted in throwing across the room. Apart from dust being repeatedly thrust down the collars of those in the workshop no-one was targeted during the two years of the disturbances, and despite the fact that some of the missiles were large and heavy and 'thrown' with considerable force there were no injuries. Attempts by the entity to 'help' were even apparent, including (in response to a joking request) surprising gifts of money in the form of £5 notes pinned on several occasions to the ceiling overnight, which together added up to over £70. (A full account of this intriguing case, which aroused great interest in the press and which has been the subject of two television programmes, is given in Fontana 1991, and a summary appears in *Is There an Afterlife?* Fontana 2005.)

An example of an Icelandic spirit who apparently stayed earthbound through a desire to have his physical remains discovered, and whose case was extensively documented by leading researchers Professors Ian Stevenson and Erlendur Haraldsson, involved a communicator who, through medium Hafsteinn Bjornsson, gave his name as Runolfur Runolfsson and claimed that he was 'looking for his leg'. Angrily and uncouthly he related that he had been carried out to sea during a storm, had drowned, and that his body on being washed ashore had been torn apart by dogs and ravens, and that when the remains were found the thighbone was missing. In addition to his name, Runolfsson gave the date of his death, his age when drowned, the name of the church where he was buried, the owner of the house where his missing bone could be found, and the fact that he had been a very tall man (facts that were all unknown to the medium and to the members of his circle).

Investigators subsequently found an unusually long thighbone hidden behind the wall in the house named by Runolfsson, and church records were uncovered that confirmed the date of Runolfsson's death and his age, together with the fact that he had been drowned and his body dismembered. In due course the bone was buried at Utskaler Church where Runolfsson's other remains were located, and Runolfsson (or rather his spirit) became a reformed character, eventually serving for some years as the medium's chief control.

It may seem odd that Runolfsson remained earthbound simply for the sake of his thighbone, but the facts suggest that overconcern for one's physical remains (which the deceased may feel effects the spirit body) may be sufficient to hold one captive in this way. It was only when Runolfsson's preoccupation with the bone was satisfied that he seems to have regained his free will and, although no longer earthbound, to have chosen to remain in contact with the medium out of gratitude.

Examples of supposedly earthbound spirits who remain close

to the earth through desire or unfinished business are relatively common. In a case discovered by Patricia Robertson of the Scottish Society for Psychical Research, which she invited me to investigate with her, two young adult sisters sharing a house together were so alarmed by distressing disturbances in their bedrooms, such as bedding being pulled forcibly from their bodies during the night, that they were forced to sleep on the ground floor and venture upstairs only in daylight. The disturbances had commenced soon after the death of an uncle who they considered had been sexually attracted to them, and in their view it was his earthbound spirit that was responsible.

Attempts to contact the spirit proved unsuccessful, but in such cases the disturbances gradually die away of their own accord, as if the spirit concerned loses interest in the living.

'Hungry ghosts'

Earthbound spirits are reported from many cultures. The Tibetan Buddhist teaching of earthbound 'hungry ghosts' is a good example. Hungry ghosts, who are said to have an existence tormented by an inability to enjoy the sensual pleasures that they see around them in the physical world, are said to bring their fate upon themselves by living greedy, selfish and sensual lives while on earth. They are described as experiencing a form of hellish existence (we have more to say about 'hell' in Chapter 6) by *seeing* things that they desperately desire yet proving unable to partake of them, rather like being thirsty and starving at a fabulous feast yet unable to swallow a morsel of food or a sip of drink. In Tibetan Buddhist iconography, hungry ghosts are symbolized as figures with tiny necks that prevent their taking nourishment, and this effectively sums up the concept. 'Hungry ghosts' would seem to belong to the third of the groups of earthbound spirits listed above, those who remain earthbound through desire, although the

Tibetan teachings concerned must of course be placed within their cultural context. Western mediumship places more emphasis upon the need to 'rescue' earthbound spirits, if they exist, than upon their unredeemable nature.

Possession by earthbound spirits

The best evidence for poltergeists comes from those cases where investigators are able to witness the phenomena for themselves under conditions that minimize the possibility for trickery or for exaggeration and misrepresentation. The Cardiff poltergeist mentioned above was one such case, and another good example is the Enfield case investigated by Playfair and Grosse and fully described in *This House is Haunted: An Investigation of the Enfield Poltergeist* (Playfair 2008). The whole subject of poltergeist hauntings is expertly surveyed by Gauld and Cornell (1979), and on the basis of the evidence available it is difficult to dismiss the reality of poltergeists or of the earthbound spirits who may be responsible. This is also true of so-called *possession* by earthbound spirits, cases in which spirits appear able to invade the consciousness of a living individual to the extent that they can become troublesome and potentially dangerous. Let's look at an example.

The victim (if we can use the term) in this case was the late Suzy Smith (see Smith 2000), a prolific author and journalist who possessed the gift of automatic writing, a mediumistic technique in which one of the hands is taken over by a supposed spirit and writes material independently of the consciousness of the medium and seemingly from the spirit. Distinguished mediums such as Leonora Piper and Geraldine Cummins have used the technique extensively, and Suzy Smith discovered her own gift after receiving a message through a ouija board telling her to 'get a pencil'. Following many fruitless attempts over several days, the pencil, held loosely in her hand, suddenly began to write as if by itself, an event she described as 'the most peculiar feeling I'd ever experienced. The hand was just writing by itself without my conscious will being involved in any way'. When she read the straggling writing she found it to be a loving message from her deceased mother, promising to write 'more next time'.

From then on, Suzy Smith sat regularly for automatic writing, but before long she found that 'intruders', who she later claimed to recognize as earthbound spirits, began to interfere, often giving information through the writing that turned out to be lies and that reminded her of 'the nasty individual who spends his time calling people on the telephone and whispering filth into their ears before they can hang up'. These intruders eventually stopped bothering her when she resolutely ignored them, all except for one annoying individual who gave his name as 'Harvey Boone'. 'Harvey' repeatedly protested his love for Suzy, and at first seemed fraudulent but harmless. Increasingly, however, he not only intruded into the automatic writing but succeeded in shutting everyone else out. Each time Suzy Smith picked up her pencil, only 'Harvey' was present, and eventually she was forced to abandon her automatic writing altogether.

However, while working on a new book some time later she relaxed with her fingers resting on the typewriter keys (a habit only too familiar to most writers awaiting inspiration) when she found her 'hands began to type slowly, seemingly of their own volition', writing material unrelated to what she wanted to write. Her mother, it appeared, was in contact, and this prompted her to start automatic writing once more, this time with the typewriter rather than a pencil. However, before long the intruders started interfering again, even seemingly 'pulling' Suzy's hands from the keys of her typewriter if she tried to concentrate on receiving messages from her mother. On the rare occasions when her mother did succeed in making contact she insisted that the intruders were not evil but 'misguided spirits ... [needing] help to learn the truth about their condition ... everyone arrives here in the same mental state in which he lived ... the opinionated person whose mind is closed to new ideas has the hardest time', arriving in the spirit world 'in more or less of a fog, which continues ... until the development of his understanding'.

Inevitably, in due course 'Harvey' also reappeared, but surprisingly insisting that this time he was ready to learn how to progress in the spirit world and to accept the help of Suzy's mother. He apologized to Suzy through the typewriter for 'all the trouble he had caused', and a few days later fell silent and Suzy heard no more from him. Suzy Smith's reputation as a writer and psychical researcher was such that it is unlikely she consciously fabricated these experiences. It is possible that a 'secondary' or 'sub-personality' of her own took over when she was in a relaxed state and that everything then came from her own unconscious, but there are objections to this.

Genuine cases of sub-personalities that supplant the central personality, even if briefly, are rare and likely to occur only in psychologically disturbed individuals who may unconsciously wish to escape from themselves or to express hitherto repressed aspects of their personalities. There is no evidence that Suzy Smith was such an individual. More common are certain kinds of mental illness in which sufferers 'hear' voices in their heads that use threatening language and that appear to be independent of themselves, but again there is no evidence that Suzy Smith suffered from mental illness or indeed that such illness manifests itself as coherent and informative automatic writing. Consequently, it seems fair to give her credit for being an objective observer of what seems to have been a mediumistic experience of troublesome earthbound spirits.

There are, in fact, examples of cases where possession is said to have been wrongly confused with mental illness. American medical doctor Carl Wickland worked for 30 years with his mediumistic wife Anna Wickland and a small home circle in an attempt to help some of his patients who consulted him about troublesome inner voices that seemed to be symptoms of mental illness, but that he thought might have originated with their attempts to contact spirits through the ouija board (Wickland 1978). The ouija (pronounced 'we-ya' from the French and German words for 'yes') board, which we encountered a moment ago in connection with Suzy Smith, consists of the letters of the alphabet in a circular arrangement around a moveable central disc on which the operator (or operators) lightly places the fingertips in the hope that the disc will slide towards letters that spell words and sentences supposedly from the spirits. There are many warnings against using the ouija board as it is said to attract earthbound spirits who can then become intrusive and possess-ive, even when the board in not being used, and Dr Wickland hypothesized that this is what may have happened to patients who could not be freed from their 'voices' by normal medical means.

Accordingly, Wickland attempted to speak to the 'voices' troubling his patients through his entranced wife, who proved successful in contacting the entities responsible. Once a dialogue was established, he then proceeded to discuss their 'behaviour' with the entities, explain the distress they were causing and persuade them to move on, both for their own good and for that of his patients. The following is an abbreviated version of one of the dialogues he records holding, through his entranced wife, with one such confused earthbound spirit who was reportedly obsessing a patient with thoughts of suicide.

WICKLAND: *Can you tell us who you are?*

SPIRIT: *No; I don't know.*

WICKLAND: *Can't you remember your name?*

SPIRIT: *I can't seem to remember anything. What is the matter with my head? It is difficult for me to think. What kind of doctor are you?*

WICKLAND: *Medical. What is your name?*

SPIRIT: *My name? Strange I can't remember my name.*

71

WICKLAND: *How long have you been dead?*

SPIRIT: *Dead? I'm not dead. I wish I were.*

WICKLAND: *Is life so unpleasant?*

SPIRIT: *Yes it is. If I am dead then it is very hard to be dead. I have tried and tried to die … Why is it I cannot die?*

WICKLAND: *There is no actual death.*

SPIRIT: *Of course there is.*

WICKLAND: *How do you know?*

SPIRIT: *I don't know anything.* [in great distress] *I want to die! Life is so dark and gloomy. I wish I could die and just forget. Why can't I die? I think sometimes I am dead, then all at once I am alive again. I want to forget all the trouble and agony that I have. Where shall I go so that I can die? … I am always pushed out into the dark again, and I go from place to place. I cannot find my home, I cannot die. Let me be free from my thoughts and this horrible darkness. Why can't I die? … give me a little light and some happiness. I have not seen either for years and years.*

Eventually Dr Wickland apparently convinced the spirit he was no longer in the material world, and helped him remember his name. It seemed he had committed suicide 17 years previously – hence his wish to die – but with Wickland's help he finally accepted he was in the afterlife, and his deceased mother was then able to contact him. She explained to Dr Wickland that her son '… had been in hell … a hell of ignorance … he thought he was alive … he has been obsessing a sensitive woman [Wickland's patient] …'.

Once contact was made between mother and son, the latter was helped to move on to the next level in his spiritual journey.

Wickland reports that once his patients were freed from their possessing earthbound entities, their improvement in psychological and physical health was remarkable. For example, after several weeks of work the patient possessed by the above entity, who had 'wasted away to a mere shadow' as her suicidal tendencies had prevented her from both eating and sleeping, gained steadily in strength and weight and health, lost her suicidal obsessions and became in Wickland's words 'entirely normal and [able to return] to live with her relatives [and resume] all her former occupations'.

Wickland's book, long regarded as a milestone in work of this kind, suggests that not only was he a caring and committed physician, he and his wife believed implicitly in their work and were devoted to it. Even though it is sometimes difficult to assess the effectiveness of psychiatric treatment, since many patients improve over time irrespective of the procedures used, it seems unlikely that for 30 years Wickland was consistently mistaken as to whether or not his patients benefited from his efforts. Often these patients were not present when he was speaking to the supposed entities through his entranced wife, which reduced the possibility that the patients were simply influenced in their recovery by hearing the entities promise to stop troubling them.

In addition, Wickland dismissed the possibility that the medium's sub-personalities were simply masquerading as the possessing entities on the grounds that '… it is manifestly impossible that Mrs Wickland should have a thousand [sub] personalities'. In addition, he tells us that 'in many cases the identity of the [possessing entity] has been unquestionably authenticated' by checking the details given by him or her with facts uncovered by subsequent research, and that the hand movements and physical pains suffered by the entranced medium, when under the control of a possessing spirit, replicated those of the possessed patient (e.g. hair-pulling, head and abdominal pains, repetitive and compulsive gestures).

A phenomenon less disturbing than possession but also sometimes associated with earthbound spirits is *overshadowing*. When overshadowed, the individual reports the seemingly undue influence of the deceased over his/her thoughts and behaviour, though without any feeling of being controlled by them, as in possession. Overshadowing seems to be due not to the actions of self-obsessed earthbound entities, hungry for the sensory physical world, but to individuals anxious to maintain a hold over those with whom they had strong emotional ties while on this earth. The deceased may, for example, wish to remain the most 'important' influences on the lives of spouses or children still on earth. Those who have experienced overshadowing tell me they wish to feel free of those responsible for the overshadowing, even though they still love them. They prefer to be in charge of their own lives rather than have the deceased interfering in them. Usually when they make this clear to the overshadowing entity – lovingly but firmly – the problem seems to fade away.

Earthbound spirits that deceive

Some of the most extensive examples of supposed earthbound spirits said to deliberately seek to deceive the living are provided by Joe Fisher in an intriguing book appropriately entitled *Hungry Ghosts* (Fisher 1990). Fisher, an experienced investigator, was so taken in by the autobiographical details given to him over a period of time by a group of communicators, through an entranced non-professional medium working with a home circle, that he even travelled from North America to Europe to verify them. Sadly, he was to find the details were nothing more than a weird mishmash of fact and fiction. The abiding impression given by Fisher is that the communicators were intent on glamourizing their earth lives by wild exaggeration, and on gaining a mental and emotional hold over those in the circle who believed in them. The apparent purpose behind this behaviour was to live their lives vicariously through mortals in order to satisfy a craving for the sensual gratification denied to them in their disembodied state.

There is some similarity here with the teaching by the early Christian Church that there are 'evil spirits' who seek to trick, tempt and corrupt the living. The Church even taught that these spirits can impersonate departed loved ones, and those fundamentalist Christian denominations, teaching that the dead remain in the grave until the last trump, argue that such impersonations explain all communications through mediums. I remember the minister of the church I attended as a boy making this point from the rostrum (even to my childish mind it seemed unacceptable), despite the fact such a belief is at variance with events in the Bible such as the appearance of the spirit of Samuel to King Saul through the mediumship of the woman from Endor (Samuel I, 28:8) and with St John's advice to '... believe not every spirit, but try the spirits whether they are of God' (First Letter of John, 4:1). It is also at variance with the teachings of Saint Augustine in his *De Cura Pro Mortuis* who assures us that 'The spirits of the dead can be sent to the living and can unveil to them the future which they themselves have learned from other spirits or angels, or by divine revelation.' Nowadays, although the Christian Church still does not formally support attempts to contact the dead, many individual churchmen are supportive of the practice (e.g. Roberts 2002).

No matter how we interpret Joe Fisher's experiences with his so-called hungry ghosts and the warnings given by St John and other saints that we should test the spirits, it seems clear that if we accept the existence of earthbound entities we should be very cautious before attempting to make contact with them.

Drop-in communicators

So-called 'drop-in' communicators are regarded as providing some of the best evidence not only for an afterlife but in some instances for the existence of earthbound spirits. The term 'drop-in' is used for communicators who arrive unannounced during sittings with mediums, and who are unknown to anyone present. Sometimes the impression is that, rather like Suzy Smith's intruder Harvey, they are earthbound spirits who force their way past less assertive communicators and give deceitful information, but in other cases they are simply lost and seeking guidance, and may supply truthful details about themselves, unknown at the time to anyone present, and that cannot therefore be dismissed as telepathy from the living. Often they seem desperate to find people with whom to communicate, and say they are attracted by the 'light' that surrounds the medium. (Good examples of drop-in communicators who provide verifiable evidence of their identities are given by Gauld 1971 and Findlay 1931).

If the information received through mediums is correct, the earth is surrounded and interpenetrated by an ever-changing multitude of the departed, as complex a mixture of the confused, the lost, the purposeful, the well-intentioned and the malicious as we find among the living. Just as our numbers on earth are continually being depleted by departures through the cemetery gates and augmented by arrivals from the maternity wards, so the surrounding multitudes are being depleted by those who move on to higher levels and augmented by arrivals through the self-same cemetery gates. Again, if the information we have is correct, many among them are would-be drop-in communicators, fully aware that they are dead, and remaining earthbound only until they have successfully communicated their survival to living family or friends. Communications from the dead appear in fact to be possible from several levels of the afterlife (although increasingly difficult for more advanced spirits who may have to 'relay' their messages through less evolved spirits), but the newly dead may be unaware of the fact and their wish to communicate may keep them earthbound for some time.

An example of a spirit earthbound by his desire to contact his family is given by Tom Harrison (Harrison 2008). The Harrison home circle met weekly for some eight years, with Tom's mother

Minnie Harrison serving as non-professional (and by all accounts outstandingly successful) medium. During one of the sittings of the circle a young boy communicated through the trumpet giving his name, his age at death (12 years), the fact that he was an only child, the name of his pet dog, the name of his village, and the address at which he had lived. In response, Tom Harrison visited the village concerned, and although the address given contained minor errors he was able to track down the family, who confirmed the tragic loss of their only child and the details he had given. Not only did Tom's visit provide the bereaved parents with great comfort, it appeared to release the boy from his earthbound condition and allow him to move on.

Unfortunately, many home circles who are visited by drop-in communicators, anxious to contact their families, prove reluctant to follow up on the information given, either because they are nervous as to the kind of reaction they might receive from sceptical families or because they fear the communicators may be of the mischievous or malicious variety, intent only on misinforming and embarrassing sitters. As in all areas of research into survival, well-conducted investigations into the incidence of drop-in communicators and into the validity of any information given by them is needed. If drop-in communicators are indeed who they say they are, one can readily imagine the desperation they may feel when nothing comes of their desire to reassure their families that they live on.

Ghosts and apparitions

Most people love ghosts stories. There is something thrilling and occasionally spine-chilling in the prospect of the dead hanging around the living, lurking on dark stairways and in empty houses, and frequenting the scenes of old sorrows and old hopes. I have always been attracted to the idea of gentle old ghosts, frail as the dust of centuries and at melancholy peace with this world and the next. But do ghosts exist and, if so, do they tell us anything of the immediate afterlife? When asked this question I used to say I have no doubt that people *see* ghosts, but what they are seeing may be the product of their own minds. Over the years I have changed my views. I have met and talked with so many sane and honest people who have seen and sometimes talked to ghosts, and I have familiarized myself with so much of the research literature on hauntings that it is hard to dismiss ghost sightings as purely subjective. In addition I have seen 'spirit' shapes materialize during séances under conditions that rule out either fraud or hallucinations (fellow investigators also present saw exactly the same things as I did). Materializations are not usually classified as ghosts, but they certainly appear to be non-physical and to have an objective existence, so share many of the features of ghosts. I have not seen an actual ghost, but during investigations I have heard disembodied voices and seen ghostly poltergeist activity. In psychical research, as in so many areas of human enquiry, there is no substitute for direct experience of this kind. Experience does not always allow us to draw definitive conclusions, but it certainly prompts us to stop dismissing the accounts of others so readily.

However, if we accept the possibility of ghosts, are they earth-bound spirits, perhaps endlessly condemned to repeat the same seemingly pointless activities? There are of course various theories that attempt to explain ghostly sightings without recourse to theories of survival. The most recent is that ultrasound (sound at frequencies above human hearing) heard at times near certain kinds of machinery can lead to hallucinatory experiences that may give the illusion of ghostly presences.

Another, more traditional explanation, is that strongly charged emotional events somehow impress themselves upon the physical environment as if upon a reel of film, which then repeatedly 'plays back' the 'memory' of them.

A third theory is that if we are in an environment thought to be haunted we tend to interpret normal phenomena – shadows, changes in temperature, unfamiliar sounds – as if they are paranormal. Yet another theory is that ghostly happenings are psychic projections by the living – for example poltergeist activity is claimed to be unconscious projections of emotional energy, typically by frustrated adolescents, that somehow causes spontaneous disturbances in the environment, while visible ghosts are 'thought forms' unconsciously projected by somebody present at the time.

Support for these theories comes from the fact that in many hauntings there seems little evidence that an actual personality is present. However, this is not true in all cases. I gave an example of apparently intelligent purposeful activity when discussing the Cardiff poltergeist haunting earlier in the chapter. This activity was frequently varied and specific to the situation rather than merely repetitive, and the same has been true of the other poltergeist cases I have investigated. Other investigators have even reported poltergeist cases in which contact has been established with the entity concerned, either through the latter's ability to rap on the wall in response to questions, by speaking through mediums, or through those individuals unaware of their mediumistic gifts (e.g. Playfair 2008). Poltergeist activity is also typically witnessed by all those present, which allows a fairer assessment to be made of whether or not an active intelligence is involved.

But what of those apparitions that actually do repeat the same actions over and over again, such as walking the same corridors or up and down the same stairs, with no signs of active intelligence? Mediums who claim to make contact with the spirits concerned often insist they do have intelligence, but are confused distraught and earthbound. Either they have failed to accept the fact of death, or they have some emotional need to remain attached to the places they knew in life, a need strong enough to render them visible at certain times.

However, this may not apply to those apparitions thought to be victims of violent crime (which is good news – it would seem a little unfair if in addition to their violent deaths they were condemned to linger as distraught shades at the scene of the crime). Unlike other apparitions, these are said to be thought forms projected through remorse from the mind of the deceased perpetrator of the crime, who is condemned repeatedly to experience the terror and pain inflicted on their victim. If so, then this process might continue until the criminal has expiated the crime through the necessary remorse (we return to the subject of expiation and remorse in Chapter 6).

Another possibility sometimes advanced is that some of these repetitive apparitions may be of those who have committed suicide, thereby making themselves their own 'victim'. However, if some apparitions are indeed linked to suicide, it seems more likely that they are earthbound because of the confused and troubled state of mind in which the suicide was committed, as in the example quoted above from one of Dr Wickland's cases. All the great spiritual traditions counsel against suicide, less from a wish to pass judgement than from concern for the troubled souls involved (things may be different for those in unbearable pain). Faiths, such as Buddhism, that believe in reincarnation (Chapter 8) often teach that, in addition to confusion in the afterlife, those who deliberately end their lives must face in their future existences the problems they sought to escape, until these problems are satisfactorily resolved.

It is not appropriate to enter into a debate on the rights and wrongs of issues such as these, but it is worth re-emphasizing that the state of mind in which one dies does appear relevant to what happens next, and to refer to the fact that a life review (Chapter 6), in the course of which one recapitulates all the events of the present life, may also include the circumstances surrounding one's departure from it.

After death communications (ADCs) without a medium

Are the communications received through the bereaved themselves, rather than through mediums, from earthbound spirits? Research suggests that some 40 per cent of bereaved individuals report receiving direct contact with deceased husbands or wives or other loved ones (*see* LaGrand 1997 and Heathcote-James 2003 for excellent collections of recent cases). The most common contact is a distinct sense of presence, often at times when the mind is elsewhere. Sometimes these may be the imagination playing tricks as a result of longings or of expectation, but humans seemingly possess the ability to be aware of the presence at least of *living* people even when they can't be seen or heard, as demonstrated by recent experiments into what is known as the *staring effect*.

The experiment is very simple and is worth explaining. Two people are placed in separate rooms joined only by a two-way mirror (a device that acts as a mirror on one side and a clear window on the other). At a given signal, audible in both rooms, the experimenter on the window side is given a random computer-generated instruction either to stare at the individual on the mirror side or to look away, while the latter responds by pressing one of two buttons to indicate if he/she senses being stared at or not. By chance we would expect these responses to be correct 50 per cent of the time, and although some experimenters have obtained only chance results, others have been successful enough to suggest that the staring effect is real (it seems likely that success may be influenced not just by the state of mind of the recipient but also that of the experimenter; the more positive he/she is, the better the results). And if some people have an awareness of the attention of an unseen living person, then a similar awareness may operate in the case of attention from the deceased.

However, an awareness of presence is not the only way in which the living report an ADC from the deceased. Visual contacts are also reported. Here is an example from my own files. The speaker is a thoughtful and transparently honest friend of mine, not given to vain imaginings. In summary, her experience was as follows.

> It was after the death of my mother. I was in the kitchen in day-light, standing at the sink facing out onto the garden, washing dishes. Suddenly I was aware of my [deceased] mother stand-ing next to me, looking well and happy. I saw her as plainly as if she was physically present. We then talked together of simple everyday things, in a matter-of-fact way. Then I was aware that she was gone.

My friend reports feeling no sense of surprise at the time. I have other cases of this kind in my files where people report the same 'ordinariness' of the experience. There is no sense of shock, and only subsequently are they puzzled that instead of expressing astonishment, or asking for details of the afterlife, they engaged only in what amounts to small talk. It seems for the duration of the experience as if time has been rewound and they are back in the old familiar relationship they enjoyed during the lifetime of the departed. In this altered state of consciousness it simply didn't occur to them to talk about deeper matters. (How often this seems to happen with psychic experiences! Frequently it is only after-wards that one wonders why an attempt was not made to ask the questions to which one really wants the answers, or even to reach out and try to touch the apparition.)

There are also many accounts of hearing the voice of the deceased as if it is objectively 'out there' rather than subjectively inside the head. So life-like are these voices that people sometimes describe turning round in amazement in an attempt to see from where the voice is coming, so sure are they that someone is there. Almost as striking are reported olfactory experiences, such as the familiar perfume used by a deceased loved one, or the distinctive aroma of a pipe or of cigar smoke. These scents are frequently described as 'overpoweringly strong'. Typically they arrive unexpectedly, or may already be in a room as one enters. Strangely, they disappear as abruptly as they arrived, leaving no trace behind.

Another ADC reported relatively frequently these days is the perplexing behaviour of electrical devices. Sometimes vacuum cleaners, radios, televisions or light bulbs regularly switch themselves on and off, even though they are checked and rechecked and no fault is found. The case for paranormality is increased if these inexplicable events follow a distinct pattern. For example, the deceased's reading lamp may come on around the time he/she was in the habit of switching it on, or it may blink on and off as if in greeting at certain times. The name Instrumental Transcommunication (ITC) is given to these electrical phenomena, which extend also to inexplicable messages received on audiotape and – more rarely – through radios, computer screens and fax machines. An impressive body of research has built up around these phenomena, which at their best appear to provide strong evidence for the afterlife. In some cases it has proved possible to dialogue briefly with the voices that intrude in radio frequencies, and a simple test I have used in the past, that successfully rules out the possibility the voices are simply stray radio transmissions, is to ask them to repeat certain words after me (see Fontana 2005 for a summary of work in this field, or Cardoso and Fontana 2004 for more detailed discussion of the research methods used).

Finally there are ADCs that arrive in dreams. The dreaming mind is perhaps more sensitive to such experiences than the waking mind, busy as the latter is with its own thoughts and external affairs. Many people report vivid dreams in which their loved ones give evidence of their continuing survival. These may simply be the creations of the dreaming mind, but there is a difference between dreaming *about* the deceased in the way we dream about other people or events, and dreaming *of* them. In my experience, and that of others who have discussed such dreams with me, when dreaming *of* a deceased person the dream becomes as immediate and coherent as waking life, unlike the rather con-fused nature of most dreaming. There is the same 'awareness of presence' that we would have if the deceased were actually present, and we are left with clear memories and a strong emotional impression that refuses to fade with the years.

Not surprisingly, after experiencing an ADC people sometimes ask me where their deceased loved ones are when they are not communicating. Are they constantly with us? Have they no other occupation? Are they visiting from higher realms? Are they aware of everything we do, even things we would prefer remained private? Can they even read our thoughts? Should we enlist their help and advice, or maybe ask forgiveness if our behaviour offends them in any way? And most importantly of all, are they earthbound?

The answers to questions of this kind must be tentative, but communicators give the impression that they are only conscious of what happens to their loved ones at significant times, such as family events. Otherwise, they are more aware of our states of mind than of our doings. The things that would have been private from them when they were alive remain private. It is a mistake to imagine they have a kind of all-seeing all-knowing omniscience that they never had during their material existence (details as to their possible whereabouts and their occupations will become clearer in later chapters). However, in the majority of cases, ADCs seem to be less associated with earthbound spirits than with spirits well aware of their present condition and anxious only to feel they have said goodbye properly to their loved ones. Usually ADCs tend to continue for a few months or a year or two before the communicator is ready to move on.

Chapter Six

·

THE FIRST PLANE
AND HADES CONDITIONS

Seven planes

Earthbound spirits are said to remain close to earth until they fully recognize the fact that they have died, discard some of their attachments to materiality and accept their need for help. They are then able to move to one of the levels of the afterlife. Is this likely to be the beautiful domain glimpsed sometimes by the dying and those in NDEs, and sometimes referred to in the literature as 'paradise conditions'? Traditions from both West and East refer to the existence of seven levels or planes above the earth, and although there may be a reassuring glimpse at or near death of one of the more exalted of these levels, it may only actually be reached after further spiritual development at the lower levels. Only those who have already achieved this spiritual development during their earth lives are said to be able to enter it directly.

In Chapter 4 we discussed the experiences of those who, like Private Dowding, die a sudden or violent death, and the experiences of what may happen to those who are earthbound. But what of those who leave this life in a better prepared and more appropriate frame of mind?

What are the seven planes?

Before addressing this question something must be said about the seven planes or levels into which the afterlife is described as being divided. Many Christians reject the idea of 'levels' in the afterlife altogether, and consider that the Scriptures teach direct entry to the kingdom of heaven for believers after death, but Christ clearly tells his disciples (John 14:2) that 'In my father's house there are many mansions' (or 'abiding places'), which seems to teach us that the afterlife must not be thought of as a single domain.

Until the Reformation in the 16th century the idea of 'levels' was an important feature of Christian thinking. Origen (185–254 CE), the leading theologian of the Church in the centuries after Christ, taught that the soul's ascent to God in the afterlife was marked by a 'hierarchy of stages' (*see* Chadwick 1966), and the idea of levels makes undoubted sense if we accept that spiritual development is possible after death.

I doubt if any of us would want to spend eternity exactly the person we are now. We may be only too aware of our short-comings, and although Christians believe that these are forgiven through Christ, many hope to learn from mistakes on earth and to continue growing in wisdom and love. We can hardly expect for-giveness to make us instantly perfect. Hence the idea of 'levels' in the afterlife which, whether we take them literally or not, are a useful way of conceptualizing something of the manner in which continuing development in the afterlife may take place.

Different names are given to these seven planes or levels in the various spiritual traditions and by different communicators, but there seems to be broad agreement that the first four of them are planes of 'form' bearing certain resemblances to life on earth, while the three upper planes are 'formless' realms of increasingly pure and rarefied consciousness. In the interests of convenience it is useful to adhere to the labels given to these seven planes by F W H Myers (of whom more later) when communicating through medium Geraldine Cummins (see Cummins 1935), as these are the ones that are perhaps best known. Beginning with the earth plane, we have in ascending order:

The Four Planes of Form

1. Earth (including earth-bound spirits)

2. Hades (or the Intermediate State, including Purgatory)

3. The Plane of Illusion (or Lower Astral)

4. The Plane of Colour (or Upper Astral or Summerland)

The Three Formless Planes
(or Planes of Pure Consciousness)

5. The Plane of Pure Flame (or Plane of Intellectual Harmony)

6. The Plane of Pure Light (or Plane of Cosmic Consciousness)

7. The Seventh Plane (Contemplation of the Supreme Mind)

These labels are useful pegs on which to hang our discussion of the seven planes, and like everything else said in this book about the afterlife should not be taken as an attempt to be definitive. But why *seven* planes? The tradition that there are seven has been with us since antiquity. It is this belief that leads us to exclaim in moments of happiness that we are in the 'seventh heaven' (though nowadays many people are for some reason more likely to claim to be 'over the moon').

The number seven has always been thought to have special spiritual significance. In the Old Testament God created the world in six days and 'rested' on the seventh (hence our seven-day week). The number seven combines three (the number of the Trinity and of heaven) and four (the number of the soul and of the earth); thus it is the number that unites the spiritual with the temporal, thereby symbolizing perfection, security, safety, rest and plenty. In Buddhism the 'seven steps of Buddha' symbolize the ascent through the seven cosmic stages beyond time and space. In Christianity there are seven gifts of the spirit, seven deadly sins, seven virtues, seven devils cast out by Christ, seven mountains in purgatory, seven major prophets, and seven sacraments (though only two are actually mentioned in the Gospels). Noah's ark came to rest on dry land after seven months, and Noah sent the dove from the ark seven days later. There are many more examples, including seven basic notes in the musical series, seven colours in the spectrum, and seven dimensions of space (four lateral, two vertical, and one central).

From the ancient Greeks onwards, a relationship has been recognized between a number's numerical value and its symbolic value, with the former concerned with quantity, and the latter with the mystic relationship between numbers and the cosmos itself. Pythagoras considered that numbers are the fundamental principle from which the whole objective world proceeds, while Plato regarded numbers as the essence of harmony, which in turn he saw as the basis both of the cosmos and of man himself. The philosophy of numbers was further developed by the Hebrews and by Christian scholars such as Aristotle and St Augustine, who saw numbers as the mechanism behind creation, the archetype in fact of the Creator himself.

Those who leave peacefully

So much, for the moment, for the seven planes. We can now return to the question of what happens to those who die peacefully. Judging by reports of NDEs and by communications through mediums, those who avoid sudden death and are at least open to the possibility of an afterlife typically are aware of making a journey, often through darkness or a tunnel, and typically towards a distant bright light. Communicators speak of a sensation of weightlessness and of great freedom, with an absence of the physical disabilities they may have been experiencing in the body. There is rarely any talk of initial fear of what lies ahead, or of regret for what is left behind. Often there is a feeling of being loved and cared for, either by the 'spirit helpers' who may be present or by some unseen force connected with the bright light. Particularly when the physical body has gone through a long period of suffering prior to death, there are often references through mediums to a subsequent loss of consciousness, either before reaching the light or immediately afterwards; a loss of consciousness said to be in the nature of a peaceful healing sleep that allows the consciousness to leave behind the troubled memories of physical suffering.

Another of Jane Sherwood's communicators, E K, informed her that he had two periods of this loss of consciousness, and that after waking from the first of them:

> I thought myself still weak and ill, but I arose from my rest feeling marvellously refreshed and happy ... I wandered ... in the something-nothing surroundings of this queer world and was unable to make sense of it. The brooding silence drugged me into unconsciousness for a long time ... When next I woke my body felt quite different, no longer frail and weak ... but vigorous ...

The late Maurice Barbanell, a respected journalist and celebrated non-professional medium, when communicating through Marie Cherrie, refers to this 'queer world' as 'like walking around in a fog ... almost like trying to stop myself day-dreaming'. Some commentators refer to it as a shadowy, dream-like condition and even describe it as *Hades*, the name given by the ancient Greeks to the underworld. However, they also suggest that it is not a place necessarily to be feared. F W H Myers, one of the founders in 1882 of the Society for Psychical Research (the first society devoted to

the scientific investigation of psychic phenomena and the possibilities of survival), was a leading figure in the history of psychical
research. Communicating post-mortem through Irish author and
dramatist Geraldine Cummins who had the gift of automatic
writing (Cummins 1984), Myers explained that Hades is the 'lowest
level' of the afterlife, and that it can be 'a place of rest, a place of
half-lights and drowsy peace ... As a man wins strength from a
long deep sleep, so did I gather that spiritual and intellectual force
I needed ...'. The individual, it seems ' ... is affected in a different
manner by this place or state on the frontiers between two lives, on
the borders of two worlds'.

These last words suggest that Hades represents not so much a
'location' as a state of mind. For each person this state of mind is
determined by his or her own life history and spiritual development. For some it may be Myers' place of 'half-lights and drowsy
peace', while for others it may be a place of haunting shadows, of
regrets and unfulfilled longings, of aching loneliness, of sadness
for lost opportunities, and of remorse for the emotional suffering
one might have caused. As such it may be connected with the life
review discussed in due course.

Those who report a 'sleep' at this time, describe Hades as followed by a joyful sense of freedom and by meetings with deceased
loved ones. The idea of 'sleep' – a state associated with the physical
body – may seem strange to us, but possibly this so-called sleep is
actually a temporary lowering of consciousness. Helen Salter, a
classical lecturer at Cambridge and a leading figures in the Society
for Psychical Research (SPR), described her death to her husband
W H Salter (Hon. Secretary of the SPR) through medium Geraldine Cummins, then added a reference to her need for rest.

[death was] such a short journey ... so incredibly easy and
painless. There was only one very brief nightmare, when I
wanted to get back into my body in order to return to you. An
instant's bad dream. That's all death was to me. After it, almost

immediately, there came the unimaginable moment – a wel-coming mother and father ... what a feeling of safety they gave me ... freedom from fear of the Unknown ... Death's exit is so simple ... Well all that grisly death meant to me was a return to my old home ...I was very tired and it has been so restful for me.

Helen's deceased father (Professor Verrall), mentioned in her account, also gave a description of her death, and made direct reference both to restful sleep and to Hades. Communicating through Geraldine Cummins he told us he and Mrs Verrall were 'summoned from another level' to meet Helen as she passed into the afterlife.

> ... it was for us the right moment on that dense level of Hades. She was struggling to... re-enter her physical body. She was distraught, did not recognize us; she only longed to go back to [her husband] but eventually we succeeded in preventing her returning and controlling again her physical body; thus we rescued her from much physical suffering and mental distress ...
>
> ... We were determined that [she] would not be kept alive by damned drugs ... Later she recognized us, and our welcome brought her peace. She sleeps well, only now and then wakes for a time then, as a small infant sleeps again.
>
> ... she just slipped out of her body, found herself above it, and struggled frantically to get back ... she experienced no pain ... I simply could not permit her the horror of pain day after day.

According to this account, Professor and Mrs Verrall were able to re-enter Hades conditions and prevent Helen Salter from return-ing to her physical body in order that they could save her from further suffering and a more painful subsequent death. Presum-ably this incident is what Helen Salter referred to as 'a very brief nightmare, when I wanted to get back into my body in order to return [to my husband]'. If Professor Verrall's account is correct this suggests that the 'spirit helpers' who visit the deathbed (Chapter 2) are sometimes able to influence the exact moment of death in the best interests of the dying.

Another example of what may be Hades conditions comes from Sir Alexander Ogston's report of his NDEs while critically ill with typhoid during the South African War at the end of the 19th century. Ogston speaks of wandering in his NDE '… under grey, sunless moonless starless skies, ever onwards to a distant gleam on the horizon, solitary but not unhappy …' (*see* Findlay 1961). Many of those who have had out-of-the-body experiences (OBEs) while fit and well, also speak of a misty environment even while still in the physical world. Clare, a friend and colleague of mine and a senior university lecturer in psychology who has succeeded in inducing an OBE consciously by a technique involving con-centrated visualization, found herself while out of her body in her own bedroom but in a dull, misty light in which the familiar objects around her seemed 'grey and dust-like'. Dr Robert Crookall quotes a number of cases in which people tell of this dull, misty light while in an OBE, and goes on to speculate that it may be because the 'energy body', instead of remaining with the physical body during an OBE, exits with and envelops the spirit, producing Hades-like conditions that make it difficult to see clearly.

Many accounts of those who have experienced Hades support the notion that it reflects the individual's state of mind. Albert Pauchard, founder and President of the Geneva Metaphysical Society, communicated after death through a non-professional medium that after his first feelings of bliss at his 'liberation' he found himself in a dark region where he walked along a seemingly endless road and was aware at one point that '… there was no sky … no depth … no perspective … no free space … There was nothing. I was alone in a desolating solitude.' When in due course Pauchard emerged from this state, spirit helpers informed him it represented 'all the depressions and despondencies' he had experienced while on earth.

Like Myers, Pauchard asserts that 'things happen in a slightly different way' for each individual (Pauchard 1987), and makes no suggestion that this dark region can be bypassed. For him it represents a learning experience during which we go through, in symbolic form, the various weaknesses in character and behaviour that emerge during our lives on earth. One of medium Jane Sherwood's communi-cators also speaks of Hades as influenced by the emotions and thoughts of those who find themselves there.

> [I spent] a long sojourn in what I think of as Hades, the place of the shade, a dim and formless world which I believe is peopled by the miasma of earth emotions and the unconscious projections of its inhabitants ...
>
> (Sherwood 1969)

Hades and purgatory

The ancient Greeks also described Hades as a place of shadows, a sunless environment where the souls of the dead exist in a languid state of torpor, and in the Old Testament the Hebrew afterlife (or *Sheol*) seems to be a similar land of shadows. There are some parallels between these descriptions of Hades and descriptions of *purgatory*, seen by various of the Christian traditions as a stage of development in which one is 'purged' of one's sins through opportunities for self examination remorse and suffering, and thus rendered fit to progress to higher planes of reality. One of the communicators reported by Ralph Harlow (a retired university professor whose interest in psychical research was aroused while a student at Harvard by no less a person than the great William James), informed him that in the afterlife 'punishment' is in reality the 'opportunity ... to rectify error'. Another communicator tells him that although 'God's love includes all ... his love cannot change a Hitler into an Albert Schweitzer' (Harlow 1968). The implication is that transformation is only accomplished through genuine repentance and atonement.

Sukie Miller (1998), in her extensive study of the various descriptions given by different cultures of the journey into the afterlife, points out however that it is only the more 'goal orientated' traditions that maintain the individual is judged in this way, on his or her earth life, rather than offered 'a natural slide from one world to the next'. This makes sense given that 'goal-orientated' cultures look to the future as well as to the present, and see the whole of existence as a process of development from what one is now to what one can potentially become – just as the child grows through education into the adult. Provided one is prepared to take the opportunity, purgatory is in fact described by communicators as a temporary state that should be welcomed with gratitude since it is a gift that enables one to be rid of earthly burdens.

Professor Geddes MacGregor, a philosopher formerly of the University of Southern California, insists that 'If we are to entertain any image of an afterlife ... the most intelligible form is on purgatorial lines', with opportunities for spiritual education and development. He reminds us that the concept of purgatory as an 'intermediate state' goes back to pre-Christian Judaism, as does the idea of saying prayers to assist those who find themselves in this state (MacGregor 1992).

The concept of purgatory indeed follows naturally from Western beliefs in atonement and redemption in the afterlife. One of Jane Sherwood's communicators informed her that:

> One cannot just lay down the burden [of the harm we may have done during our earth life] with a sigh of relief and go on free of it ... the mischief is in us, a dark cloud at the heart of our emotional being ... it has to be cured.
>
> (Sherwood 1962)

He assures us, however, this should not involve one in 'brooding' about the past. The soul must give itself to the new life in which it finds itself. One of the most helpful pieces of advice he receives from an advanced soul who descends to purgatory to help him is that '... one has got to adjust to what one is ... and accept one's being ... and patiently and cheerfully ... try to find the real man behind the façade'. This involves accepting the wrong one has done, recognizing the effect it has had upon others, and recognizing what this wrong has made of oneself.

Despite the fact that the concept of purgatory was accepted by the early fathers of the Church such as Clement of Alexandria and Origen, and that in contemporary times those with a strong belief in life after death tend to believe that 'rewards and punishments will be meted out in the afterlife' (*see* Boyd and Zimbardo 2006), it is sometimes argued that it lacks biblical support, as forgiveness is granted through faith alone. However, it is not correct that purgatory lacks biblical support. St Matthew refers to the fact that sins (except those against the Holy Spirit) can be forgiven '... in the world to come' (Matthew 12:32), a truth acknowledged by Harlow's communicator who insists that death does not make saints of sinners. If we take into the afterlife the person we are now (and if we do not, how can 'we' be said to survive?), then we take with us our failings as well as our successes.

Pope Gregory the Great, pope from 590 to 604 CE, did most to clarify the concept that purgatory is a place of redemption, and the first papal decree on the subject followed (somewhat belatedly) in 1439. The decree pronounced that those who die in 'perfect contrition' enter directly into the kingdom of heaven, while all others carry their sins into the afterlife, where 'temporal' (to do with earthly matters) sins earn a spell in purgatory, provided one is a believer, and 'mortal' sins (to do with spiritual matters) earn damnation – of which more in a moment. The ancient Greeks had somewhat similar ideas, regarding Hades as an opportunity for purgation and *Tartarus* as hell or the place of the damned.

For the medieval Church, purgatory was a decidedly unpleasant place, involving harrowing and remorseful visits to the scenes of earthly sins or the repetition of tormenting tasks symbolically connected to these sins. However, the sufferings concerned were rendered bearable by the ministrations of angels and by the certainty of eventual admittance to heaven. Furthermore, pious acts in earthly life such as pilgrimages could gain merit that reduced the stay in purgatory. Perhaps not surprisingly, the concept of purgatory gave medieval writers and artists imaginative scope to outdo each other in the portrayal of sadistic scenes of torture and similar nastiness. According to an early text, even a drop of sweat from a sufferer in purgatory would 'burn through the palm of a living hand' (see Watts 1954). However, such portrayals may have been intended symbolically rather than literally, since it is difficult to represent pictorially the profound emotional suffering said to be felt by those in purgatory when they experience at first hand the distress they have caused to others. But the portrayals may also have been intended to depict the process of re-education, since in medieval times it was believed that education was inseparable from punishment, even to the extent of beating the devil out of small children.

One of the most extended descriptions of purgatory is by the Italian poet Dante Alighieri (1265–1321), who portrayed it in his *Divina Commedia* as a circular mountain rising in a series of ledges on each of which are the various groups of repentant sinners, from those with the heaviest sins at the bottom to those nearest to heaven at the top. Dante was not only a great poet and scholar (learned in philosophy, astronomy, natural science and history) but also a visionary, and there is some suggestion that he drew not only upon this scholarship but upon his mystical insights when describing the next world. His description of purgatory is of a place at once joyful (since one is bound for heaven) but melancholic (since acute contrition is necessary to purge away sin). Penitential rituals are performed, and eventually there is a seven-fold pardon and baptism by water and by fire (Dante 2008 edition).

The concept of hell

If purgatory is regarded as a place of redemption in which the negative aspects of one's earth life are progressively recognized and discarded, what of hell? In the Christian tradition concepts of hell have changed over the years, but to the medieval mind hell was a place of eternal torment, an everlasting punishment for mortal sins (a belief still seemingly held by some fundamentalist Christian denominations). St Matthew however, in the verse referred to earlier, makes clear there is only one sin for which there is no forgiveness, namely the sin against the Holy Spirit. He does not tell us the nature of this sin and there have been many attempts by theologians to do so, the consensus being that it is condemning as evil those things that are manifestly good (and thus taking the devil's side against God). But another possible interpretation is that the sin against the Holy Spirit is a total and complete rejection of the existence of God. This rejection puts one beyond the possibility of forgiveness, since if one does not believe in God one does not believe in God's forgiveness and therefore is unable to receive it. This interpretation suggests that the sin against the Holy Spirit is an ongoing process rather than a single act.

Some support for this view may come from St Mark who tells us that 'he that shall blaspheme against the Holy Spirit hath never forgiveness but is in danger of eternal damnation' (Mark 3:29). The use of the words 'in danger of eternal damnation' may imply that this danger might end if blasphemy is replaced by sincere repentance and by openness to the Holy Spirit. To attempt an imperfect human analogy, we could say that unless one is prepared to recognize and take a proffered cure, one cannot be healed.

Origen, mentioned earlier, taught that damnation was based on the self-condemnation of those who deliberately turned away from God, though ultimately all souls would be reunited with God. St Isaac the Syrian put it that 'It is wrong to imagine that sinners in hell are cut off from the love of God' to which the Greek Orthodox scholar Father Kallistos Ware adds:

> Divine love is everywhere and rejects no one. But we on our side are free to reject divine love ... the more final our rejection the more bitter our suffering.

He also insists that:

> If anyone is in hell it is not because God has imprisoned him there, but because that is where he himself has chosen to be ...
> it is rightly said that the doors of hell are locked *on the inside*.
>
> (Ware 1979, original italics)

This seems to summarize much of the current Christian attitude towards hell, which regards hell (originally *Gehenna*, from Hinnom, a valley outside Jerusalem where animal sacrifices were burnt) as a state of mind rather than a place of quasi-physical torment, a state of mind that consists of the complete absence of God and of the spiritual transformation that can follow death. Nothing, it is argued, could be more hellish than the despair and desolation to which this separation gives rise. If the human ego believes only in itself, it creates an insurmountable obstacle to its own redemption.

This concept of hell is supported by the argument that a loving God would not have created men and women only to consign them to everlasting damnation. Christ, when dying on the cross, asks for God's forgiveness on those responsible for his crucifixion, and during his life counselled his listeners to 'render unto no man evil for evil', a teaching that conflicts with the idea of *eternal* damnation for even the worst evildoer.

In Acts 24.15 we are told 'there shall be a resurrection both of the just and the unjust', while in John 5:28 Jesus tells us that the good will be raised 'unto the resurrection of life; and they that have done ill unto the resurrection of judgement', which again avoids mention of damnation. The symbolic fire of hell may indeed be everlasting but this does not mean that even the unjust are fated to remain everlastingly in its flames.

FWH Myers, communicating through Geraldine Cummins, implies that hell is in fact an extreme form of purgatory where 'the wicked experience' the sufferings they have caused to others in a dark place created by their own memories and imaginings while on earth. In order to 'evolve' they must go 'deeper into their dark world' or return to earth where they will find themselves powerless and frustrated. They can, however, be helped by more evolved beings or by the 'actual destruction of the dark part of their souls' (*see* Cummins 1935).

The concept of hell in other religions

The idea that hell does not imply eternal damnation or annihilation also occurs in the other great world religions, although Tibetan Buddhism in particular outdoes even medieval Christianity in its descriptions of the torments of hell – or rather of hells, since Tibetan Buddhism holds that at least 18 exist, including cold hells of shivering wretchedness and hot hells of barbecued unpleasantness for all those whose store of bad karma outweighs their store of good. There is no belief in forgiveness by a divine being during earth life, only of attempting to achieve good karma and, if possible, the enlightenment consequent upon recognizing the illusory nature of the physical world and of one's own selfish ego. However, Tibetan Buddhism does insist that, like everything on earth and in the planes of form, hell is not permanent. Once bad karma is paid for, one is reborn in this world with the hope of making a better job of things. One of the many celestial Buddhas, Buddha Tsitigarbharaj, is also said to visit hell and offer help with the process of redemption for all who call upon him, thus shortening the sojourn in whichever of the hells one is unfortunate enough to find oneself.

Many of the traditions that go to make up Hinduism see rebirth as following almost immediately after death, and therefore have little to say about the lower planes of the afterlife. As in Tibetan Buddhism, the nature of rebirth is seen to depend upon karma from previous lives, and in extreme cases can be in the form of an animal rather than that of a human being. The wheel of death and rebirth continues to turn until we become 'enlightened' by recognizing (and actually experiencing) that our indwelling soul, the *Atman*, is in reality one with *Brahman*, the Absolute First Cause. Once released from this wheel we return to Brahman. Neither Hinduism nor Buddhism place the same emphasis upon the survival of individuality as do the major Western traditions (Christianity, Islam and Judaism) or upon a perfected, fully sanctified relationship with God.

However, for all the great traditions, Western and Eastern alike, experiences in the afterlife or in future rebirths are seen as consequences of our doings in the present life. This realization that there is no escape from our own actions or from the rejection of spiritual realities seems to have been with us from early recorded history. In the Egyptian Papyrus of Ani, dating from approximately 1290 BCE, the *ab* (the heart or seat of conscience) of the deceased is pictured being weighed against a feather in the Hall of Maat, the god of justice. If the heart is heavier this indicates a sinful nature and it then falls down to Amenet, the crocodile-headed god, who devours it (whether this implies permanent extinction or not is unclear, but the prospect hardly sounds attractive).

Even the ancient Greeks, with their misty poetic descriptions of Hades, believed that at the sub-Hades level Tartarus existed for the souls of the really wicked, who faced punishments of ingenious nastiness appropriate to their earthly misdeeds. For example, King Tantalus, for trying to deceive the gods, was condemned to spend his time under trees whose fruit was blown out of reach every time he tried to satisfy his hunger, and near water that vanished whenever he tried to drink; Sisyphus, for failing to keep a promise to the god of the underworld, was condemned to roll a great stone uphill that rolled down again every time he was about to reach the top; Tityus, for attacking Apollo's mother, was chained to a rock while vultures devoured his liver; Ixio, for trying to seduce Hera the wife of Zeus, was bound to a wheel that revolved over a hot fire; and the Danaids (the daughters of Danaus), for murdering their husbands, were condemned to stand eternally upright and to attempt to fill broken water jars from broken pitchers.

This world as hell?

A rather intriguing belief sometimes encountered is that hell is in fact the very world in which we now live. The belief was associated particularly with the gnostic Christian heresy of Catharism that flourished in the Languedoc area of France in the 12th and early 13th centuries before being suppressed by the so-called Albigensian Crusades initiated by Pope Innocent III and King Philippe Augustus of France. Catharism taught that this world was created not by God but by a lesser spirit (a *demiurge*) who, after being expelled from heaven, constructed earth as a very imperfect copy of the heavenly realms. The Cathars considered that in view of its imperfect creation this world is innately sinful, and that our souls are trapped within it by imprisonment in our physical bodies. They also rebelled against the excesses and corruption of the Catholic Church, and sought to live the austere and selfless life of the early Christians, rejecting the priesthood and believing each person can have direct access to God.

Dr Arthur Guirdham (e.g. Guirdham 1980), a psychiatrist who was led by a number of psychic experiences to take an active research interest in Catharism, tells us that it included the belief that opposing forces of good and evil, of spirit and matter, are engaged in a universal war with each other, a belief also found in Mithraism, the religion of the Roman Empire before Christianity. There are also signs of it in Greek philosophers such as Epictetus and Democritus and even Pythagoras and Plato, and in theologians such as Origen, Plotinus and Porphyry. For the Cathars, the aim of the spiritual life was to break free of the sinful prison of this world. After death, advanced souls, who have broken free from all earthly attachments, go to higher planes of the afterlife, while those that are less developed experience a period of reflection and learning in the lower planes before being drawn back to this world by ties of affection to their particular 'Group Soul' (souls with whom their destiny is inextricably linked across many lifetimes).

The belief that this world is hell finds no echoes in the world's great religions, which all see this life as a valuable learning experience and (apart from Buddhism) as the creation of a loving God rather than of a wicked demigod. Consequently when towards the end of his life I met Dr Guirdham, a man of great compassion, sincerity and scholarship and one of the 20th century's foremost experts on Gnosticism, I was unable to agree with him that our world was created by a demiurge. However I was more than ready to accept that a sizeable proportion of the human race seem intent on turning it into a hell.

The life review

At some point in the Hades experience the individual is said to experience the 'life review' (first mentioned in Chapter 2), which can even occur – in part at least – just before death. Most of us will have come across the story that the drowning man sees the whole of his past life flash before him, and as mentioned earlier a colleague and close friend of mine who narrowly escaped drowning described it as happening to him 'simultaneously and panoramically', as did one of the communicators quoted by Lysa Moskowiz Mateu (1999) who claimed that

> Every feeling, thought, and experience I had ever felt in my entire life I saw in one fell scoop … [in] a flash of light … the love I had shared and the people I had touched … and the pain I had caused.

Similar accounts are given in some NDEs. But how can the whole of one's past life flash before one in the brief interval between life and death or soon after death? The answer would seem to be that, even if only briefly, one is outside time, with a bird's-eye view of the whole of what has led up to that moment. The life review thus becomes a single experience, a single experience that includes moreover both the physical and the emotional constituents of what one's life has meant. It is as if we all have this complete record within us, and at the threshold of death, or shortly afterwards, we begin the task of learning the necessary lessons from it.

Heath and Klimo (2006) report that the life review (together with the self-judgement that it prompts) is the 'most consistent and universal stage described [in accounts of the afterlife], regardless of the culture or era. From ancient Egyptian writings and the Islamic book of the dead to [communications through modern mediums]' there are frequent reports that souls must go through this experience before they can proceed to the higher planes. Communicators who have reached these higher planes frequently speak, in addition, of a second life review that takes place in the so-called Plane of Colour (Chapter 9) and that is far more leisurely and reflective than the first review, allowing the soul to learn all the lessons of earth life and finally to lay to rest all the regrets and disappointments that may be involved.

What might the learning from both life reviews actually involve? Primarily that each moment of our lives is forever present, together with the consequences of our every action. We are not merely *influenced* by past events, we are in part the sum total of those events. Normally we think of our 'self' as what we are in the here and now, a 30- or 40-year-old man or woman perhaps. The life review indicates that although the body displays the badge of our years, our essential self is outside time, with each life experience an equally valid part of the whole. We are, in the present moment, our childhood, our adolescence, and our adulthood. A mystical concept perhaps, but one that like all mystical concepts we should not dismiss too lightly, particularly if we find it resonates with our innate sense of possibilities. And try telling someone who has been through a life review, when near death, that the experience was not what he or she thought it to be. And try telling them they are no more than the fleeting instant of the here and now. Some experiences bring clarity and certainty to those who have them, and it is not for those without such experiences to attempt to dictate what they mean.

Descriptions of the life review indicate that it is not like *thinking about* what has gone before, it is like being back within the experiences and emotions concerned, like entering a picture book instead of just turning the pages. We are told that this past life review, which in most cases seems to happen soon after death rather than before, is essential if we are to learn the lessons of our life on earth. It thus becomes a necessary part of any purgatorial experience. Only by seeing a record of our lives, and the consequences of our thoughts and actions for others as well as for ourselves, are we able to approach self-understanding.

Communicators give no consistent information on how long is spent in Hades (if time has any meaning in our terms) or in purgatory, which may be because as Pauchard, quoted above, indicates, 'things happen in a slightly different way' for each individual. In his case he reports he spent a 'long sojourn there', but tells us nothing of the transition from Hades to the next plane. In fact, as with the question of how long is spent in Hades, we are given no consistent details on how and when this transition takes place. Presumably, if Hades is for many a place of rest, increasing clarity may begin to dawn when this rest is complete and the first life review and any purgatorial experiences have taken place. Thus there may be no obvious transition as such, but just the dispersal of the Hades mists and an opening out of the next plane.

Chapter Seven

·

THE PLANE OF ILLUSION

Expectations and the Plane of Illusion

The human mind would be unlikely to retain any sanity if in the afterlife it was abruptly translated into an existence devoid of any of the familiar landmarks by which it orientates itself in the physical world. The departed can only make sense of their new experiences if they find themselves in a world resembling in important respects the one left behind, just as we expect a familiar world to greet us when we open our eyes each morning. Hades conditions are sufficiently recognizable to meet this requirement, even if only at a featureless dream-like level, but by the time the individual reaches the next stage of development, the so-called Plane of Illusion, he or she will have a much greater awareness of the surroundings and expect to comprehend far more of what is experienced. The fact that this expectation is apparently realized explains why the Plane of Illusion is referred to by some leading thinkers such as Oxford philosopher Professor H H Price as a *mental world* (Price 1995).

Actually even this term is a little misleading, as it suggests the Plane of Illusion is a level *entirely* created by the mind. If it were, then each person would be imprisoned within his or her own mental creation, with no possibility of shared experience. Since communicators are adamant that shared experience exists, we must suppose that there is an objective coherent potential 'out there' which is the same for all, but which is in some ways sensitive to the wishes and expectations of the individual who can – within certain limits – create a personal illusory reality within it which others can see and share. This means that the term 'Plane of Illusion' should not be taken to imply an entirely personal world, with each of us lost in a self-contained reality of our own creation.

The descriptions available to us suggest that each individual gravitates towards those locations where there are individuals of a like mind to him or herself. Those who love nature and a peaceful world find themselves in dimensions where the minds of others have, unconsciously and consciously, helped create just such an environment. Those who are drawn to towns and cities go where others have helped create illusory towns and cities and so on. FWH Myers, through Geraldine Cummins, puts it that in the 'Plane of Illusion' we 'seek out' those people to whom we were drawn when on earth, and our new surroundings depend to a certain extent upon them. Each community builds up its own 'little world', even creating its own 'time and space', which enables the individual to visit 'communities of people like-minded to him or herself that existed two or three hundred years ago', since people may remain in this plane for a long time in human terms before moving on to the next plane or perhaps to reincarnation on earth (*see* Cummins 1935).

This would explain why the Plane of Illusion is sometimes described as a place of many contrasts, ranging from communities living quietly among peaceful landscapes and blessed with social harmony on the one hand to communities immersed in hectic activity and even serious if friendly competition on the other. Having come through Hades/purgatory, dark areas of strife and hatred and negativity will have been left behind, although some communicators speak of being taken back to visit these areas and finding a frightening maelstrom of crime and iniquity, where many of those present are still driven by greed and the lust for money or for power. The communicators tell us that those who inhabit such places are still in a form of hell as they have refused to learn the lessons of their earth lives, and that they will remain there until they recognize their plight and seek help.

This should not be taken to imply that those who have reached the Plane of Illusion are now free from their own defects of personality. Much development still remains to be done. But they have begun the process of identifying and repenting and learning from these defects, and realizing their potential for moving behind the selfish concerns that dominate material existence.

The nature of the Plane of Illusion

We are told that even though there are different communities in the Plane of Illusion it is possible for individuals to have intercommunity dealings, though this can sometimes cause confusion as each community represents a different kind of reality. The late Maurice Barbanell, reporting through medium Marie Cherrie, tells us that there is '... some confusion with realities, so much depends on what you want to see. [It is] difficult to keep readjusting'. Having met his deceased mother in the afterlife he goes on to report that 'Mother's reality is not my reality', and elsewhere he stresses that:

> ... it's a strange thing this reality. You've got to realize constantly that you'll only see what you want to see and so you've to make a conscious effort to broaden the field and sometimes you're seduced by what you want to see.

Subsequently he explains that this 'Can be confusing. I am groping towards my own reality, [I] can't be sure if I have achieved it yet.

I know how easy it is to see what you want to see ... [It is a] comfortable trap but still a trap.' There is an ever-present need to exercise 'will-power and discipline', but 'Concentration [is] not always easy'. If your concentration fails, 'Other people's reality intrudes' and you become confused. However he recognizes that 'Maybe there's an easier way. [I] Notice others who have been here longer [are] not having the same difficulty' (*see* Cherrie 1987).

The fact that individuals 'create' their own realities makes possible sense of the descriptions of the Plane of Illusion that include references to people wearing clothes and living in houses and indulging in some of the pleasures enjoyed on earth. In 1916 one of England's greatest scientists, Sir Oliver Lodge, published *Raymond: or Life and Death* following the tragic death of his son Raymond, serving in France with the South Lancashire Regiment during the First World War. After his death, 'Raymond' communicated through two leading mediums, Vout Peters and Gladys Leonard, and provided facts that could not have been known to the mediums and that convinced Lodge and his family, and many readers of the book, that Raymond had survived physical death.

Not surprisingly, the publication of *Raymond: or Life and Death* disturbed those sceptics opposed to any suggestion that physical death is not the end of us. Unable to find fault with the evidence provided by 'Raymond' through the two mediums, they resorted to ridiculing his descriptions of the afterlife, in particular his reference to the fact that one of the soldiers who had died with him in the trenches seemed able to smoke a cigar. We still hear sceptics (most of whom have not read the book) use the cigar episode to dismiss any suggestion that the communications from 'Raymond' were anything other than flights of fantasy by the mediums. But if we read what 'Raymond' actually said about cigars, we see that it is consistent with what others tell us of the initial levels of the afterlife, i.e. that one can obtain seemingly objective facsimiles of objects found on earth.

Through medium Gladys Leonard, 'Raymond' is reported as saying:

A chap came over the other day, who *would* have a cigar ... [I] thought they would never be able to provide that ... But there are laboratories over here and they manufacture all sorts of things in them ... Not out of solid matter but out of essences ... It's not the same as on the earth but they were able to manufacture what looked like a cigar ... But when [he] began to smoke it, he didn't think so much of it ... he had four altogether, and now he doesn't look at one.

(Lodge 1916)

On earth, cigars are manufactured through the manipulation of matter, but in the Plane of Illusion 'Raymond' claims they are made from what he calls 'essences' (perhaps his term for the objective coherent potential from which the mind may create its afterlife illusions). FWH Myers, through Geraldine Cummins (*see* Cummins 1984), provides further detail, claiming that objects are fashioned unconsciously (and presumably also consciously) from what he calls the 'plastic ether' of which the Plane of Illusion is composed. He tells us that this 'plastic ether' also yields light, blue skies, breezes, water, vegetation – in fact very much the natural world as we find it in this life. Presumably it is also used to create clothes for those who wish to wear them (we return to the question of clothes below), and houses for those who wish to live in them.

FWH Myers, in a second volume of his communications through Geraldine Cummins (*see* Cummins, 1935) tells us that it is even possible for beings to eat, drink, sleep, and to experience 'sexual passion' in the Plane of Illusion if they wish. And if we go back for a moment to the subject of smoking, it is worth noting that Maurice Barbanell reports through medium Marie Cherrie that his old friend, fellow journalist Hannan Swaffer, whom he meets in the afterlife:

[is] still smoking, even over here ... Filthy habit ... Ash down his front ... Think he only does it to shock and be an individualist. This is in character with the man.

The idea that things can be 'manufactured' on request also seems to apply to 'house-building'. In theory this bears some comparison with what happens on earth. Even on earth we could, given the necessary strength and skills, build a house for ourselves, but instead we go to architects and builders because they have better ideas and skills than we do. If there are indeed houses in the afterlife, then it seems not unreasonable to suppose that help in 'manufacturing' them might be sought from those better equipped with the necessary creative mental abilities. Some people may simply have more of the expertise needed to create illusions than others.

Many of the descriptions we are given of the Plane of Illusion are in fact not so outrageous as we might at first suppose, if it is indeed a place where thought can manipulate the 'environment' more directly than it can on earth. Even on earth, scientific research shows that thought alone can sometimes produce changes in the material world to a small but measurable extent (*see* e.g. Jahn and Dunne 1987), and in an afterlife composed of more subtle 'energy' with which the mind can interact, the results could be on a much larger scale (even though, as we shall see in due course, of an apparently transitory nature).

This may suggest that the Plane of Illusion may be composed of a subtler version of the quantum reality that underlies our own visible world. If it does, then maybe there is more of a continuum between this world and the next than we might suppose. We are even told that in the next world some people open shops and that others enjoy shopping in them, which adds to the impression that the Plane of Illusion may be a form of make-believe existence in which individuals continue to think of themselves as they were on earth, an existence in which, as

Barbanell tells us, the ability to stay sufficiently concentrated is vital if one is to remain within one's own reality. Those who are unable or unwilling to do so become drawn into the fantasies of others – with the result that, for example, they visit the 'shops' created by these fantasies and purchase their fantasy 'goods', presumably paying for them with money that is as unreal as the cigars to which Raymond refers.

Consequently it seems important to concentrate on one's own reality. A young woman who tells us in a communication that she is living with deceased members of her family explains that if they fail to concentrate sufficiently they find that rooms previously in their house have puzzlingly ceased to exist. This may point to the importance of developing concentration while on earth through techniques such as meditation, which have been highly developed within all the great spiritual traditions. The more focused and disciplined our thinking in this world, then the better prepared we may be for the next life. Meditation is also likely to help develop the calm, tranquil state of mind that we have seen appears so important at the moment of death itself.

Survival of a body?

All that we have said so far in this chapter presupposes the survival of the body, at least in some form or other. How credible is this? The great religious traditions all state or imply that bodies of some kind continue to exist. Christianity tells us that Christ appeared after his death on no fewer than four occasions, on one of them to 'above five hundred brethren at once' (1 Corinthians 15:5ff), and demonstrated that his resurrected body resembled his physical body even to the extent of bearing the wounds inflicted upon him while on the Cross (John 20:27). St Paul tells the faithful that they are united with Christ 'by the likeness of his death' and will be united with him 'by the likeness of his resurrection' (Romans 6:5).

The 4th-century St Cyril, Bishop of Jerusalem and recognized in the 19th century as a Doctor of the Church in recognition of his scholarship, wrote that this body 'would not be in its present state of weakness ... for it will be made spiritual and will become something marvellous'.

Other religions also have physical resurrection traditions. Bodhidarma, the patriarch responsible for introducing Zen Buddhism to China, is said to have become homesick for India near the end of his life, and to have been seen after his death by a traveller on one of the high Himalayan passes walking back to India carrying just one of his sandals. We are told that on hearing the traveller's news Bodhidarma's followers opened the sealed cave in which he was buried and found it empty save for one sandal. For ordinary mortals we are of course not discussing actual physical resurrection, but the fact that physical resurrection does feature in religious traditions indicates the mystical importance attached to the human form as a reflection of a universal archetype (we return to the subject of archetypes in Chapter 10), a point emphasized in Genesis 1:26–27 where we are told man was created in God's own image.

Apparitions, whether of the dead or of the living, are reportedly seen in a facsimile of their physical bodies, even down to wearing the clothes worn by these bodies. People often seem more surprised by the references to clothes than they do by references to the apparitions themselves, and use the idea of clothes as a reason for dismissing everything as the observer's imagination. However, if the afterlife is indeed a world of thought then clothes would seem no more impossible than any other mental artefact. In Dr Wiltse's well-known account of his near-death experience (Myers 1903 gives the full transcript) he reported that on leaving his body he was conscious of his nakedness, and that his consequent embarrassment resulted in his immediately finding himself clothed. His embarrassment was sufficient, it seems, to create the thought form of a suit of clothes. Those who report seeing the spirit leaving the body at death sometimes comment on its nudity, since at that point the dying probably have more pressing concerns on their minds than embarrassment at nakedness.

Professor James Hyslop, professor of logic and ethics at Columbia University and an outstanding investigator of the paranormal, suggested that clothes are in fact pictures used by the deceased to identify themselves, and thus are '… mental phenomena masquerading as realities of another kind, but masquerading only because the subconscious of the [human observer] misunderstands their nature' (Hyslop 1918). This accords with the view many years earlier by the great Swedish scientist and sage Emanuel Swedenborg (Swedenborg 1966), but against this view is the fact that Dr Wiltse was as convinced of the 'reality' of his clothing as any human observer would presumably have been, and it is difficult to avoid the conclusion that objects apparently seem as 'real' to those in the lower levels of the afterlife as objects in our world seem to us.

Bodily senses and needs

A communication from the deceased Myers was quoted earlier to the effect that in the Plane of Illusion it is possible 'to eat and drink and even to sleep and experience "sexual passion" [for those who] wish'. Comments such as this, which are also made by other communicators, suggest not only the existence of a body but of bodily senses, and many communicators do in fact also refer to sight, hearing, touch and to holding conversations (verbally and telepathically) with other spirits. Critics sometimes argue that we cannot have senses without an actual physical body, but this is a rather naïve argument since we are not talking about 'seeing' or 'hearing' or 'touching' actual physical objects in the afterlife, any more than we are talking about doing so when we use our 'senses' in dreams.

More puzzling is the fact that individuals report possessing their senses when apparently out of their physical bodies in OBEs and NDEs but while remaining in the physical world. However, as they also tell us their hands pass through physical objects and their bodies pass through walls it seems clear that they are not relating to material objects with their actual material senses. We have to propose instead what has traditionally been called 'mindsight' (*see* Ring 1999), a direct mental awareness of the environment rather than an awareness mediated through any physical organ.

Another question sometimes asked is if spirits have a 'body' do they also have internal organs? We are told for example that there are those who enjoy the sensations of eating and drinking, but does this imply digestion as well? And if – as the deceased Myers is reported as saying – some people also enjoy sexual passion, does this imply functioning sexual organs? Such topics are usually avoided by communicators, but we do have possible insights from the phenomena reported at physical séances. Tom Harrison, who kept a careful record over many years of the physical phenomena witnessed at the small home circle held weekly with his mother as the non-professional medium, tells us that on one occasion a regular member of the circle, Dr Brittain Jones FRCS, medical superintendent of Middlesborough General Hospital and a firm believer in the reality of the phenomena witnessed by the circle, confirmed the presence of a pulse in one of the materializations by feeling her wrist, at his own request, in a good red light and while the medium Minnie Harrison was deeply entranced (*see* Harrison 2008).

The circumstances under which the sittings were held (a small room, a good red light, eight experienced sitters, no hidden entrances) together with Dr Brittain's own expertise, effectively rule out the possibility that he was duped into holding the wrist of a clandestine accomplice. But if he felt a pulse, does this mean the materialization also had a cardiovascular system? If, as we are told, materializations such as those at the Harrison circle are in effect formed and made visible with ectoplasm extruded from the medium's body (Tom Harrison's communicators informed him that the reason they appeared in 'robes' was that these were easier to materialize from ectoplasm than clothes), does this mean the astral body is not just an outer form but an exact facsimile of the physical body, complete with internal organs?

Communicators inform us that after death the astral body, as if in response to its own intrinsic 'blueprint', reverts not only to full health but to the prime of life (or in the case of those who die in childhood to a time when they would have been in the prime of life). They also tell us that nevertheless they can choose to appear to the living in the form in which they are best remembered, old or young. This suggests the astral body enjoys a somewhat fluid existence in which form is always responsive to thought. Thus, if the astral body does carry a 'blueprint' of its physical self, then if the individual believes he or she has internal organs then maybe they have. This possibility seems supported by the fact that many mediums complain of feeling in their own bodies the aches and pains suffered by the deceased who communicate through them since some of the deceased appear under the illusion they are still suffering from the maladies of their days on earth, an illusion they only lose when reassured to the contrary.

What of the sex act itself and of emotional relationships between men and women? 'Sexual passion' as Myers disarmingly calls it, implies that along with the other senses the sensation of sexual arousal may also persist in the astral body. This tells us nothing about the mechanics involved, but an attempt to offer these details is by Robert Monroe, although his experiences occurred not after death but during some of the many OBEs in which he reports visiting the 'astral planes'. In the first of these he found himself, to his surprise, 'filled with a great desire for sexual satisfaction', which faded almost immediately on returning to his body. The same desire again overwhelmed him on his next OBE, only to disappear as before on re-entry to his physical body, leaving him feeling guilty and disgusted with himself. However in a subsequent OBE he found that when a woman in her astral body moved close to him there was 'a quick, momentary flash of the sex charge'.

After a number of similar experiences at other times he concluded that the sexual act experienced in the physical body:

> ... seems but a pale imitation or a feeble attempt to duplicate this very intimate [experience when out of the body] which is [nevertheless] not at all sexual as we understand the term. In the physical drive for sexual union, it is as if we are somehow remembering dimly that emotional peak [that occurs when out of the body,] and translating it into a sexual act.
>
> (Monroe 1972).

We do not know how representative Monroe's experiences were, or at what level of the afterlife they occurred, or even whether the women he met were in the afterlife or merely out of their bodies. No actual bodily contact seems to have taken place, though possibly if, like food and drink, those in the afterlife think contact is necessary it may happen. Be this as it may, communicators insist that the emotion of love survives death, and that lovers are reunited and continue their loving relationships. However, Christ informed his listeners that the resurrected 'neither marry nor are given in marriage' (Luke 20:35). Marriage, as a legal bond, seems to belong to this world only. In the afterlife individuals are drawn together solely through love, and it may be that a man or a woman can love – and be loved by – several people at the same time, with all concerned untroubled by possessiveness or jealousy.

In response to a question we put to the communicators during the Scole investigation we were told in fact that they 'live in each other's consciousness, in other words individual consciousness, particularly at the higher levels of the afterlife, seems not to be isolated from other minds as it is in this world. The bonds of love between people are therefore much closer and function at a much deeper and less selfish level. Close relationships formed on earth can be renewed and deepened, while new relationships with those of like mind can be formed. If ultimate reality really is love, as the great spiritual traditions assure us, we can assume that at each successive level of the afterlife individuals draw closer and closer together until the bond of love is fully realized.

A final question on the subject of the 'body' that is sometimes asked is why should a body be needed at all in the afterlife? Surely pure consciousness would be preferable? Eastern religions certainly teach that as the spirit moves up through successive planes of the afterlife the body and the worlds of form are progressively left behind and there is indeed an eventual entry into the formless realms of pure consciousness – ideas that are discussed later in the book. But in the Western traditions there is insistent emphasis on the body (at one time it was even held that resurrection occurs only at the 'last trump', at which point the physical body actually rises 'incorruptible' from the grave and goes forward to judgement), which is sometimes regarded as if it has a mystical purpose of its own.

Greek philosophers and artists in the flowering of ancient Greek culture (4th and 3rd centuries BCE) regarded the body as the physical reflection of ideal spiritual forms made manifest by the gods in the heavenly realms. Greek sculpture, which has never been bettered for its depiction of the male and female forms, was an attempt by artists to capture these ideal forms, both as representations of the beauty of the gods and as gifts for them. We may wonder how these sculptors obtained the creative ability to improve on earthly beauty in their work, and the answer might be that this work was done in an altered state of consciousness during which they had access to visions of perfection. Whether this was the case or not, the extent to which the human form has inspired artists of both sexes through the centuries does add to the possibility that it may have a purpose greater than its short span of material existence.

Like it or not, it seems that if survival is a fact we may have to accept that, initially at least, it involves a body, though as we shall see in the next chapter a body that is said to become increasingly idealized and etherealized as we develop spiritually, and to draw closer to the beauty that the Greek sculptors strove so hard to capture in all its perfection.

Chapter Eight

.

REINCARNATION

Ties with the earth

At this point we come to another aspect of the afterlife, namely possible rebirth back on earth. This is the appropriate place at which to consider rebirth, as communicators lead us to believe that, if it is a reality, it normally occurs only for individuals in the planes of form, who still have strong ties with earth. The further one progresses away from earth the more difficult it becomes to return, and in any case increasing spiritual development renders it less and less likely that one would want or need to return. By the time one reaches the Plane of Colour, we are told that reincarnation is a rarity.

Is there evidence for reincarnation?

Belief in a return to this world immediately after death, or after a period in the next world, is widespread. Many people argue that reincarnation makes good sense because if we live after death then surely we must have lived before birth, and that as human life plays such an important role in spiritual development it is unlikely we would be given only one chance at it. Another argument is that as abilities, advantages and opportunities vary so widely from person to person then, assuming the universe gives us all a fair deal, it follows that they must be a consequence of our own behaviour in previous lives.

These arguments have their strengths, yet they also have their weaknesses. The fact that we may live after death has no relevance to whether or not we existed before birth, at least in any meaningful sense of personal identity. The molecules of which our bodies are composed would have existed, and our souls may have existed as part of some dormant, undifferentiated potential, but that is not the same thing as self-conscious individual existence. And the argument that human life is so important we are surely likely to be given more than one chance at it is less compelling if it is true that human life goes on developing in the various levels of the afterlife. Earth life may simply be the bottom step on a long staircase.

The argument from fairness is also not really convincing. If 'fairness' is the governing factor behind the universe then logically everyone would have to start their first lives with identical abilities and be given identical advantages and opportunities during each subsequent lifetime, with the result that individuality and diversity would never arise. All we would have would be an army of human clones, without choice or free will. As diversity is clearly a fact of human experience, it hardly seems that human concepts of what is 'fair' and what is 'unfair' have relevance to any debate on reincarnation. Ultimately everything may have its own individual purpose, and ultimately everything may work out equably in the afterlife, with those who have suffered misfortunes in this life revealed as having learnt more as a result and as having made better progress than those who have had smoother pathways, but the notion that diversity is 'caused' by behaviour in previous lives does not bear real scrutiny. It also carries certain moral and social dangers in that it can lead people to be regarded by their fellow men and women as responsible for their own misfortunes, which reminds us that we need to be on very sure ground before accepting it.

An argument that also throws doubt on reincarnation is that it is not compatible with the fact that the world's population has exploded so dramatically in recent decades. There are as many people alive in the world today as there were in all the centuries prior to industrialization, and the world's population is expected to increase by another 25 per cent (over two billion) by the middle of the present century. The standard reply to this is that people reincarnate more rapidly nowadays than ever before, but we have no way of knowing if this is the case (or indeed what might be the explanation should it prove to be the case). The argument that reincarnation is not compatible with the population explosion remains effectively unanswered.

Past-life memories

There is, however, a practical reason for accepting possible reincarnation. Many people have claimed to remember their past lives, sometimes producing obscure and detailed memories that seem to check out with the facts. A good example is the well-known writer Joan Grant, who claimed that her novels were 'far memories' of her own previous lives, recalled while her mind was in an attentive and receptive state (*see* Grant 1956). Memories of what seem to be past lives have also come spontaneously from small children, reportedly too young to have learnt the details concerned by normal means (typically these memories fade as the child grows older), and have also come from adults when undergoing hypnotic regression. Adult memories can also surface in recurring dreams or in *déja-vu* experiences in which a place that is seen for the first time conveys an inexplicable yet unmistakable conviction of familiarity, or in response to consciousness-changing procedures such as the Christos technique which combines sensory disorientation and vivid mental imagery (*see* Glaskin 1974 and 1978).

People also report strong and unaccountable feelings of being drawn to specific periods of history, or of having spontaneous convictions that old objects or places are connected with their own past, or that a stranger encountered for the first time is known from a previous life. It is sometimes said that we all have memories of past lives hidden deep within our unconscious, and that it only requires a trigger of some kind for them to be recalled. It is even maintained that in the afterlife we are able to review some of these past lives and continue to learn the lessons from them.

Of all these apparent memories, those recalled under hypnotic regression are among the most intriguing. Once having established the hypnotic trance, it is relatively easy for the psychologist trained in hypnosis to regress the client back into childhood in an attempt to uncover hidden early memories that may play a part in causing current psychological problems. The hypnotist may, for example, suggest that the client is now descending a staircase that goes down deeper and deeper into the past until in due course the latter is imaginatively back in the experiences of early childhood. If the regression is also to involve supposed past-life memories, the client is then taken further and further back, to a time many years before birth, and then asked to describe what is seen and what is taking place. If the regression has been successful, the client will now, with eyes closed, proceed to give detailed descriptions of what seems to be a quite different lifetime from the present one. Prompted by questions from the hypnotist, he or she is often able to give details of age, sex, clothing, habitation, occupation and family, and perhaps to name the year, the name of the king or queen or president, and what is happening nationally.

As a psychologist qualified in hypnosis I have used past-life regression with consenting colleagues, and been regressed myself. There is no doubt that the experience is exceptionally realistic and – as with dreams – apparently outside one's conscious control. The things that occur in the course of it appear to be totally unexpected, as if indeed a past life is unfolding around one. The surroundings, the adventures, one's own sense of identity all seem self-evidently real – more so even than dreams since one feels fully conscious, and the events have a coherence and logicality typically absent in the dream world.

The most extensive piece of research into past-life regression was carried out by the late Dr Helen Wambach, a psychologist on the staff of the Monmouth Medical Centre in New Jersey USA. Helen Wambach's research (Wambach 1979a and 1979b) involved hypnotizing a number of groups of volunteers (over 1,000 volunteers in total), taking them back beyond birth and inviting them subsequently to fill in extensive questionnaires on the historical details of their experiences. As a scientist, Dr Wambach was interested primarily in the extent to which these details could be verified against known facts relevant to the periods to which volunteers claimed to have regressed.

When Wambach's results were analyzed they revealed distinct and unexpected patterns. For example, it was found that although the volunteer participants were allowed to regress to any one of ten given historical periods from the last 4,000 years, the graph of periods chosen replicated the graph of population densities during these periods. In other words, more people were found to have regressed to periods of higher population than to periods of lower, although no details of population densities were given to them before the experiment. Another interesting finding was that although more people usually claim, when asked, that they would prefer to be male than female if they had a choice, the balance of the sexes among the regressed lives showed only a very small preponderance of male incarnations over female (50.3 per cent as opposed to 49.7 per cent, much as in real life). Many males regressed to lives as females and vice versa. Among other important findings was that, contrary to popular misconceptions, very few people claimed to have regressed to lives of any consequence or even particularly happy lives, and no-one claimed to have been a known historical figure. In the overwhelming majority of cases the lives concerned were reported as obscure and even humble (70 per cent reported lives in the lower classes, 23 per cent in the middle classes, and only 7 per cent in the upper classes). In addition, the details given of such things as clothing, footwear, architecture, food, domestic utensils and climate were found to be accurate for the historical periods involved, even though volunteers claimed to have no special knowledge of them. Out of the 1,088 participants, only 11 produced results that showed discrepancies with the known historical facts.

These findings appear favourable to the possibility of reincarnation. Nevertheless some reservations exist. Wambach's volunteer participants may have known more about the periods to which they regressed than they realized (information long forgotten is often recovered under hypnosis). In addition, many subjects undergoing group hypnosis may not go very deeply into the hypnotic state, and may have consciously chosen to go to a period which interested them and about which they had some knowledge. It is also possible that Wambach's methods of analyzing the questionnaire responses were faulty (though the analysis concerned was sufficiently straightforward to render this unlikely). Another possibility is that our knowledge of the domestic details of life in the historical periods to which participants regressed may not be extensive enough for reliable assessments to be made of the accuracy of participants' responses.

Nevertheless, it remains difficult to account for Dr Wambach's results by these or any other normal explanations. She also gathered details from her participants of their experiences of 'death' and of the afterlife state encountered between the lives to which they had regressed and their present incarnation, and found that 90 per cent of participants reported that the act of dying was pleasant and peaceful, and that they were taken to a tranquil afterlife where they were able to learn the lessons of their earth life. Only when they had learnt these lessons did they have to face rebirth, and only 26 per cent reported having looked forward to the experience. The remaining 64 per cent regarded their rebirth as an unhappy and even frightening prospect – very much against Wambach's expectations. Thus their supposed afterlife experiences matched those that have been reported in our previous chapters. This seems impressive, but we do not know how much they may have read on the nature of the afterlife before participating in Wambach's research. The very fact that they had volunteered to take part does suggest they may have had a particular interest in the subject. And it is possible that their expressed unhappiness at the prospect of rebirth may have been influenced by recollections of distressing incidents in their present lives.

On balance Wambach's results are very interesting, but too many questions remain unanswered for us to conclude that they present an unanswerable case for reincarnation.

Past-life memories in young children

Another approach to past-life memories is to work with young children who speak of having lived before their present lives. If these early memories appear before children have had opportunities to learn any of the details of which they speak, and if these details turn out to be correct, then we certainly have cause to think paranormality may be involved. Research into children reporting what appear to be past-life memories is particularly associated with the late Professor Ian Stevenson of the University of Virginia, who in company with colleagues including Professor Erlendur Haraldsson of the University of Iceland, spent many years on the task (see e.g. Stevenson 1974, 1987).

Ian Stevenson found most of his samples of children in India and Sri Lanka, countries with large Hindu and Buddhist communities where reincarnation or rebirth are taken as facts of life, and was able to build up an extensive dossier of data which allowed him to conclude that, in addition to remembering correct details relevant to apparent past lives (lives lived in distant towns that the children had never visited), a few of the children had birthmarks that corresponded to the injuries said to have caused their deaths in these previous incarnations.

Stevenson never claimed that his work proved reincarnation to be a fact. There is always the possibility, however remote, that a very young child may have overheard adults speaking of the death of someone from another town or village, and unconsciously internalized the details and come to believe they applied to him or herself. There is also the equally remote possibility that they may have been deliberately schooled in the memories concerned by parents anxious to attract attention in cultures where past-life memories are taken very seriously. Unlikely as these explanations are, they might conceivably be stretched to explain those instances of children who have found their way unaided around the streets of the strange towns where they claim to have lived, and who have apparently recognized the members of 'their' past-life families.

I doubt if anyone who has studied Professor Stevenson's meticulous work with the care it deserves would accept these alternative explanations. Unless one persists in dismissing paranormality as a possible explanation under any circumstances, the more feasible explanation is that some of the children he investigated were in fact able to give details of past lives they could not have known by normal means. However, this is not necessarily a clinching argument for reincarnation. The question is, did these reported memories relate to their own past lives or were the children picking up memories of *other* people's lives, rather in the way that mediums do? Those who accept the possibility of reincarnation are likely to see the scales as weighted in favour of the children's own past lives, while those inclined to reject the possibility will see them as tipped in the opposite direction. With a question as finely balanced as this, personal preference may determine which way the conclusion goes.

Can cryptomnesia explain past-life memories?

The same question arises of course with adults who recall past lives under hypnosis. Are they also picking up memories that belong to people other than themselves? However, another issue arises to further complicate matters. There seems little doubt that in the course of past-life regression people do recall accurate historical details which they insist were previously unknown to them. But were they really unknown? There is an argument that a process known as cryptomnesia was actually responsible. The term *cryptomnesia* refers to the recall of facts without any attendant recall of having learnt them. We absorb an enormous amount of knowledge during our lifetimes, and although most of it is apparently forgotten without trace it may nevertheless be stored deep in the unconscious. Particularly under the imaginative experience of hypnotic regressions these hidden memories may surface and weave themselves into past-life fantasies. Crypto-amnesia is in fact the recall of memories without the realization that they are memories.

Cryptomnesia may also be at work when supposed past-life memories occur spontaneously. A picture, an object, or a person seen for the first time may appear hauntingly familiar although we feel certain we have never encountered it or them before. Immediately we may wonder if a past life is involved. However, experiences such as this can be explained by those who prefer a normal explanation as 'recognition without recall'. We *recognize* that a seemingly unfamiliar experience strikes a chord of memory, but we fail to *recall* this because it resembles a similar experi-ence earlier in our present life. Once cryptoamnesis occurs, the imagination may unconsciously provide seemingly convincing elaborations, much as happens in dreams, and this may suggest that the experience is paranormal whereas in fact it may be nothing of the sort.

Although cryptomnesia may explain some supposed past-life memories, it is unlikely to explain them all. Human memory is notoriously fallible, but it seems unlikely that individuals who provide a range of accurate and extensive details, some of them obscure and technical, connected to supposed previous lives would have no recollection of having studied these details during their present lifetimes. In addition, past-life memories sometimes appear as if they might be the source of deep-seated psychological problems in the present lifetime. A number of accounts by psychiatrists exist of clients who, while under hypnosis, have recalled seemingly traumatic past-life memories of this kind. The hypothesis advanced to account for such cases is that we store past-life memories deep in our unconscious, and that although we do not recall them they may affect important aspects of our present lives. We saw earlier that past-life memories may possibly be responsible for birthmarks on the bodies of young children, and it is also hypothesized that irrational fears and dislikes such as agoraphobia, claustrophobia and hydrophobia may also have their origins in unfortunate experiences in previous lives.

One of the first books to describe the way in which uncovering past-life memories seems to help recovery from irrational fears and other psychological problems was by novelist Joan Grant (mentioned earlier) and her psychiatrist husband Denys Kelsey (Grant and Kelsey 1969). Having employed hypnosis for regressing patients to childhood in order to uncover early traumatic memories from their present lives, Kelsey agreed to his wife's suggestion that he try past-life regression with patients whose problems were still troubling them. Results convinced him not only of the reality of past lives (in his words 'regression can have a sense of immediacy which is enveloping and absolute') but of the role they play in the incidence of distressing psychological symptoms in current lifetimes. A number of psychiatrists who have subsequently tried similar methods have reported findings that agree with those of Kelsey (e.g. Weiss 1988, Fopre 1980, Williston and Johnstone 1988).

The difficulty in drawing firm conclusions from work of this kind is that the very act of *seeming* to find the cause of a psychological or physical problem can help the process of healing, partly because the sufferer now feels he or she 'understands' the problem better and consequently worries less about it, and partly because the ability of mind and body to heal themselves can be strengthened if the sufferer develops a more optimistic outlook on the chances of recovery. Thus the simple fact of believing that the root cause of a problem lies in past lives can have a strong curative effect, even though the 'past life' revealed under hypnosis may be no more than fantasy. Nevertheless we cannot, in the light of present knowledge, rule out the fact that something more than fantasy may be involved. If reincarnation is a fact, and if it has a purpose within the context of psychological and spiritual development, then it makes sense to suppose that our past lives may influence our present lives, even to the extent of causing long-standing psychological problems.

Certainly the various pieces of evidence for reincarnation deserve to be taken seriously, even if they allow for alternative explanations. Perhaps the strongest of these, if we accept that some of the details of past lives reported by children or adults cannot reasonably be explained by normal means, is the one mentioned earlier, namely that occasionally some individuals prove able to tap into the memories of the deceased, rather as psychometrists appear able to tap into their memories by holding objects that once belonged to them. In addition, mediums have told me that if they were not experienced at telling the difference, they could sometimes be deceived into believing that the memories of those who communicate through them are actually memories of their own.

In my own work with mediums I have never received information from communicators that insist reincarnation is an inevitable fact of life. Professor Archie Roy, Montague Keen and I once carried out a questionnaire survey of the views of mediums on a number of issues relating to their work, and found in fact that many of them claimed to be unconvinced of the reality of reincarnation, which suggests that they also may not have received references to it in the course of their work. On the other hand, FWH Myers, communicating through Geraldine Cummins (*see* Cummins 1935), indicated that reincarnation does occur, though he agreed it becomes increasingly difficult to return to earth the higher one ascends through the levels of the afterlife.

Obviously the evidence seems fairly evenly balanced between arguments for and against reincarnation. Space does not allow us to go more deeply into these arguments, but for those who wish to do so there are a number of sources available for study. One of the most comprehensive is the extensive volume by Head and Cranston (1977), which also contains extracts from the references made by many distinguished Western writers to previous lives and the possibility of previous lives. Christie-Murray (1988) also gives a good, if shorter, survey of the relevant arguments. Numerous collections of accounts, supplied by people who profess to remember past lives, have also appeared over the years and continue to appear. Some are supported by what appears to be good evidence such as historical and domestic details, some of them authenticated, as with Ian Stevenson's children, by interviews with still living people who apparently knew the subject in his or her previous life (e.g. Cockell 1993 – *see also* Fiore 1980, Williston and Johnstone 1988).

If I had to offer my own conclusion on the subject, I would say that the evidence tends to incline towards reincarnation, but only for some people. Much may depend on the individual's readiness to learn the lessons of the present life, both while living it and after death, and also on his or her readiness to progress spiritually in the afterlife and loosen the ties to material existence. Head and Cranston (whose book is referenced above) also accept the possibility of reincarnation, but take the view that it would only be what they call our 'native aptitudes' and not our acquired skills, knowledge, and memories that would be incarnated. The former they refer to as our individuality and the latter our personality. I disagree with this. If our acquired characteristics are not carried from one life to the next then this rules out the possibility of progress over the span of lifetimes. Each lifetime would start from the same develop-mental point as the previous one. And if personality and memory are not carried forward into the next life then it is hard to see how 'we' could be said to have survived.

Reincarnation in Tibetan Buddhism

Up to now we have only looked at evidence produced in the Western world, but the majority of the world's population follow Eastern religions that accept reincarnation as a matter of course for all, except the very few who attain full enlightenment during their earth lives. The Eastern religion currently attracting most attention in the West is of course Buddhism, and among Buddhist schools it is Tibetan Buddhism that has the most comprehensive teachings on reincarnation (or rebirth as Tibetan Buddhists also call it). So it is now to Tibetan Buddhism that we turn, not in search of further evidence for the reality of reincarnation but for how Tibetan beliefs compare with Western beliefs, and for the way in which these Tibetan beliefs deal with the concept of *karma* which in Eastern religions and in Western New Age philosophies is believed to be a major influence upon what happens from lifetime to lifetime.

Central to Tibetan Buddhist teachings is that only in this world do we have a chance to meet the challenges and the choices between good and evil that enable us to make spiritual progress, and ultimately to achieve enlightenment and see beyond the illusory nature of material existence, renouncing as a consequence the transitory pleasures both of this life and of the next lifetime (see Dalai Lama 2000). Even if we accumulate an abundant store of karmic merit by living a virtuous and compassionate life, and as a result find ourselves in the heavenly realms after death, we have to return to earth once this store is exhausted because in the perfection of the heavenly realms (possibly analogous to the Plane of Colour described in the next chapter) we no longer have the challenges necessary to progress to full enlightenment and step off the wheel of birth and death and enter the ineffable state of nirvana.

So sure are Tibetan Buddhists of the reality of reincarnation that when a high lama dies a search begins shortly after his death for his new incarnation, in the belief that even if he has attained the chance to enter nirvana he will voluntarily return instead to earth to continue teaching others. It is believed that before his death he will have given some indication of where he will be reborn, and when the time is deemed right his senior monks will set out for the locality concerned, taking with them his personal effects (e.g. his robes, his bowl, his sandals and his mala or meditation beads) with the aim of finding a young child born since his death who proves able to pick out these objects from a collection of similar ones. When the child is found, he may also show signs of joy on recognizing the senior monks. Subsequently, when he is a little older, he is taken, with his parents' consent, back to the monastery to begin his life as a monk all over again. It is said that the young child's readiness to adapt to monastic life and to spiritual practices, and the success with which he assumes once more his exalted role, is living proof that that he is the reborn lama. The Dalai Lama, one of the great spiritual teachers of our time and hailed as the rebirth of Chenreizig, the fully enlightened Buddha of Compassion, is probably the best example of this.

Critics have suggested a nefarious motive behind this, namely that by taking and controlling a young child the senior monks ensure the continuation of their own power within the monastery. It is also argued that independent witnesses are not present to observe the process of selection, and to note if the child really does spontaneously choose the objects used by the deceased lama, or whether these are placed in a position (such as close proximity to the child) that ensures they will be picked up first. Objections of this kind risk underestimating the sincerity and the sagacity of dedicated Buddhist monks, to say nothing of underestimating the success of their ability to identify young children who will later prove to be not only successful community leaders but highly gifted scholars and spiritual teachers. It is true that we must not overlook the effectiveness of the intensely personal and focused education given to the child, commenced when he is very young and conducted in an enclosed, highly structured and ritualized environment, but the system seems to have served Tibetan Buddhism well for many centuries, and it would be unwise to dismiss it simply on the grounds it defies the logic of the rational Western mind.

The *Tibetan Book of the Dead* and reincarnation

Tibetan Buddhism makes a clear distinction between the terms *rebirth* and *reincarnation*. The former is simply the act of being reborn, said to be the inescapable lot of all living beings, while *reincarnation* is the power possessed by rare and highly advanced individuals to be able to choose their future birth. The doctrine of rebirth is best known in the West through the *Tibetan Book of the Dead* (the Bardo Thodol), which we met in Chapter 3 and which is one of the most comprehensive accounts of the process of dying and of the interlude in the afterlife and of rebirth available in world literature. The Bardo Thodol is read by the Tibetan

Buddhist lama to the dying person both before death and for three days after death (a period when the consciousness is believed to be still closely associated with the body) in order to provide instructions on what is happening to the consciousness at these times. In effect it is a guidebook instructing the dying on the appropriate state of mind at death and on coping with the experiences that follow.

First published in English in 1927, the *Tibetan Book of the Dead* (*see* Evans-Wentz 1960) was a great favourite with Carl Jung, who valued it not only for the psychological insights it provides but for the emphasis it places upon the paradoxical 'both-and' concept that he argued underlies much of reality (i.e. many aspects of reality, such as thoughts, are both real and unreal). Thus the experiences of the deceased in the initial stage of the afterlife (the *bardo*) are said to be *both* projections of the deceased's own mind *and* real. To quote from the commentary that Jung wrote to introduce the book, 'The background of this unusual book is not the niggardly European 'either-or' but a magnificently affirmative 'both-and'. (Jung 1960). In a more recent translation of the same text (Thurman 1994) we find the words, 'Mind, this bright process of intelligence, in one way exists and another way does not.'

The Bardo Thodol tells us that after death the deceased remains in the *bardo* for a symbolic period of 49 days during which he or she is said to experience hallucinations created by their actions and experiences while on earth, and to see illusory visions of 'peaceful' and 'wrathful' deities that represent the personified forms respectively of the most elevated human sentiments (said to emanate from the emotions) and the reasoned and intellectual impulses (said to emanate from the mind). However, although illusory in one sense, in another these visionary deities are 'real' in that they are embodiments of genuine divine forces. The task of the deceased is to recognize that ultimately our own minds are not separate from these forces. If the deceased recognizes this fundamental truth he or she is able to remain undistracted by the illusory environment and to focus upon the Clear Light (the *Dharma-Kaya*) of Pure Reality which is visible at this time, and upon the realization that this Clear Light is one's own true nature and that one is therefore identical with Pure Reality.

The Bardo Thodol puts it that:

> ... experiencing the Radiance of the Clear Light of Pure Reality. Recognize it. ... thy present intellect, in real nature void, not formed into anything as regards characteristics or colour, naturally void, is the very Reality, the All-good ... Thine own intellect, which is now voidness, yet not to be regarded as the voidness of nothingness, but as being the intellect itself, unobstructed, shining, thrilling, and blissful, is the very consciousness, the All-good Buddha.

Inevitably there are problems for any translator in capturing the exact meaning of the Tibetan text. The word 'intellect' used in the above quotation means not just the intelligent mind but a faculty that is literally *all-knowing*. Thus in the *bardo* we are said to be given the chance to recognize that we already possess this all-knowing mind, and that furthermore the Pure Reality of which it is an expression embraces or is all things. Should the deceased fail to realize his or her oneness with Pure Reality, additional opportunities exist in the form of 'Five Wisdom Lights', said to be the five pure propensities of existence that emanate from Pure Reality. If however these opportunities are missed, the deceased is left to wander in the *bardo* until the realization dawns that the body he or she is occupying is illusory, which prompts an overwhelming desire to possess a physical body once more, leading to the wish to seek inevitable rebirth in the physical world.

Good karma from the previous life will lead to a favourable rebirth, while bad karma will lead to an unfavourable one – perhaps not even as a human being since Buddhism teaches that a human life is rare and difficult to obtain. A particularly unfavourable rebirth may be as an animal or as a 'hungry ghost' (an existence equated, as we saw in Chapter 5, with the Western concept of earthbound spirits) or, at the very worst, in the hell realms.

In Buddhist and other Eastern traditions *karma* is said to be the cumulative effect of our actions and thoughts in our earthly lives, with bad karma incurring a karmic debt that must ultimately be repaid on earth or in a lower form of rebirth, but the principle of karma raises certain difficulties for the Western mind. If karma determines many of the experiences that await us, this would seem to limit free will. Moreover, in our modern, highly complex and socially, economically and geographically mobile society, it is hard to conceive how each individual life could be so organized that everyone meets the consequences of actions performed in previous lives or the opportunities for redeeming them with meritorious acts. And if my bad karma earns me ill-treatment in this lifetime, do the people who ill-treat me earn good or bad karma as a result, since they may in fact have assisted me to repay a karmic debt, which would be a meritorious act even if their motivation is bad?

Such questions may seem simplistic, but presumably some mechanism would be needed to ensure that each individual out of the teeming billions in the world is presented with the life experiences his or her karma warrants. Even if we accept the modern interpretation that karma is simply making the best of whatever set of circumstances occur, we still have to recognize the need for some kind of overall plan or pattern, otherwise we might wait many lifetimes before appropriate karmic opportunities present themselves.

One explanation would be that all things are possible for a god who created the complexities of the universe, but Buddhists prefer not to refer back to a creator god and a first cause, preferring instead to speak of 'beginningless time'. Differences over the reality of a creator god and of divine forgiveness, as opposed to the expiation of karmic debts, do in fact represent one of the major differences between Buddhism and Christianity. It is true that reincarnation was taught within the Platonic system of Greek philosophy (5th to 4th century BCE) and tolerated in Christianity up to the year 553 CE (at which point it was formally rejected by the Council of Constantinople) but it has never played an important or even generally acceptable part in Christian philosophy or theology.

However, the more closely we study the Bardo Thodol, the more we recognize that in itself it possesses similarities with the Plane of Illusion. Once again we are confronted with an illusory mental world in which experiences are created from the memories, the attachments, aversions and ignorance that the unenlightened mind brings with it from earth. The hallucinations seen in the *bardo* are 'real' in that they represent genuine mental propensities on the part of the viewer, while at the same time they are 'unreal' in that they evidence these propensities in their crude, undeveloped form. Even visions such as the peaceful and the wrathful deities are seen only through the veil of the viewer's ignorance, and not as emanations from the Ultimate Reality from which all things arise and to which all things eventually return.

In Buddhism all things, including ourselves, are both what they appear to be and at the same time not what they appear to be. They exist but they are not self-existing – i.e. they are not complete and unique entities in themselves. Each person, in fact each created thing, contains all of Ultimate Reality in itself. Some Western mystics have made a similar point. The 18th/19th-century poet and mystic William Blake is a good example, writing that when our eyes are truly open it is possible:

To see a world in a grain of sand
And heaven in a wild flower,
Hold infinity in the palm of your hand
And eternity in an hour.

(From *Auguries of Innocence* 1803)

The truth he is trying to communicate is that Ultimate Reality is a Unity, and if all things are expressions of this Unity, then rather as each part of a modern hologram contains the entire hologram, all created things – even a grain of sand – contain Ultimate Reality. This raises profound issues that are beyond the scope of this chapter, but we shall touch on them again in Chapter 10.

The bardo as illusion

The *bardo* teachings are comparable to those of the West in that they insist the mind plays a major role in creating the experiences met with in the initial stages of the afterlife. However, there is no mention of the houses, countryside, trees and flowers in the *bardo* that we find in the Western literature because such things were not a feature of Tibetan culture, and even had they been the Bardo Thodol would have dismissed them as illusory memories of earth life, and insisted that instead of being attracted to them they should be disregarded so that the mind can concentrate upon the reality behind appearances.

In the light of these cultural differences, the Bardo Thodol should not be taken as a literal description of what a Westerner might encounter after death. If a Westerner were to find him or herself in the Buddhist *bardo* the result would be not only confusion but probably terror. Imagine dying in a Kentish village with white houses and apple orchards and the drowsy sunshine of a summer afternoon and then finding oneself in a rocky windswept landscape peopled with wrathful Tibetan deities brandishing bloodstained swords. The Westerner could hardly be expected to realize that these visions are in fact helpful symbols, well known to Tibetans, of the forces that destroy ignorance. Similarly, imagine the Tibetan villager trying to make sense of an afterlife of white houses and apple orchards and a British summer.

The references in the Bardo Thodol to the 'Pure Light' do

however have echoes in Western experiences. Westerners who report near-death experiences, or who communicate after death, frequently refer to a bright light in the distance as they move through Hades conditions or through a tunnel immediately after death. Professor Kenneth Ring, formerly of the University of Connecticut and one of the investigators who has done much to give the NDE scientific credibility (*see* e.g. Ring 1984) puts it that what is seen in the NDE is 'light', and that this light is in fact:

> the soul's own effulgence, incomparable, radiant, splendid, primordial and unconditioned. This light is both a symbol and an apogee of the NDE ... the universally recognized expression of our divine core manifesting itself in spiritual experience. The light is one's pure soul essence, undefiled by human character ...
>
> (Ring 1990)

The 'primordial light' in Ring's view is thus said to be 'universally recognized' (i.e. in Tibetan and Western and all other cultures) as the 'expression of our divine core', of our divinely created spiritual essence. Both in NDEs and in many communications from the deceased the light is also said to 'permeate' the scenery, and we might speculate that it is this divine light that, when refracted through the illusions in the mind of the observer, creates the imaginary ('imaginal' is a term often used to refer to experiences that are partly real, partly imaginary) scenery of the afterlife, rather as the light of the sun produces coloured images on the walls and floor when it streams through a stained-glass window.

However, the Bardo Thodol appears to differ from Western traditions when it teaches that it is our failure to recognize the true nature of this Clear Light and to remain undistracted by the illusory images projected by our own minds that prevents us from transcending the *bardo* and passing into the ineffable reality of nirvana. It also tells us that if, having missed the opportunity provided by the Clear Light, we also fail to recognize the true nature of the five lesser lights, the 'Wisdom Lights' of the purified propensities of existence, we even miss the opportunity of taking a propitious rebirth in this world or in another dimension. Having missed these opportunities we then become distracted by the 'dull blue light' said to emanate from the material world, and this distraction, along with the desire for a body, is responsible for drawing us back to rebirth on earth. By contrast, Western spiritual traditions and Western communicators lay stress not upon once-and-for-all opportunities such as these but upon gradual learning and development.

Tibetan Buddhism takes the view that rebirth is not restricted to the earth realms. Those with exceptionally good karma may be reborn in the heavenly realm, perhaps analogous to the Plane of Colour dealt with in the next chapter. However, as we have seen, the heavenly realm is not regarded as especially desirable as it does not offer the challenges and problems necessary if further progress to enlightenment is to be made. Consequently, advanced individuals decline the prospect of heaven in order to be reborn on earth, which may tie in with the information from Myers, quoted earlier, that reincarnation becomes more difficult once one enters the Plane of Colour.

Tibetan Buddhist tradition, together with Eastern religions generally, makes little reference to the possibilities for learning and development in the afterlife. Learning and development seem for them to be features only of this world, although an exception is the Pure Land or *Jodo-Shu* tradition that believes devotion to the Buddha Amitabha – Japanese Amida – leads to rebirth in the Pure Land (the first of the formless realms) where the step to final enlightenment is easier than on earth. Some smaller Buddhist sects have similar beliefs in connection with the paradise realms of other Buddhas. Apart from Jodo-Shu, Buddhism seems therefore to be rather at variance with the Western view that spiritual progress is an essential feature of the afterlife. But on one thing both East and West seem agreed. Whether through reincarnation or through the life review and other leaning opportunities in the afterlife, death does not make us perfect. Professor Ken Ring emphasizes this when writing of the beautiful light and other visions sometimes experienced in NDEs.

> The light appears to shine on all with its unconditionally accepting radiance, and everyone seems to enter in an atmosphere of all-pervasive pure love, [but this does not] make all things well after death, regardless of how we have lived.

The light and the visions 'may ... dissolve our personal sense of sin', but we cannot be absolved from the responsibility for our own lives. At this very moment we are 'writing the script for our own after-death [experiences]'. How we have lived 'will be evident – perhaps painfully so – after death ... What we see is a representation of what we have been in the depths of our psyche'. By way of illustration he quotes from a poem by mystic and teacher Kabir that emphasizes the importance for our lives after death of the way in which we live in the here and now. One of Kabir's verses puts it that:

> What is found now is found then.
> If you find nothing now,
> you will simply end up with an apartment
> in the City of Death.

Chapter Nine

·

THE PLANE OF COLOUR
(SUMMERLAND)

Movement between planes

Movement between the seven planes of the afterlife seems to
depend upon spiritual progress. Thus earthbound spirits move on
when they recognize the reality of survival and break free from
over-attachment to the material world; those in purgatory when
they have reviewed their earth lives and atoned for their mistakes;
and those in the Plane of Illusion when they have seen through the
illusory nature of their existence and seek higher meaning and
purpose to existence. Some communicators tell us, however, that
those who are unable to make this progress and who remain
attracted to the material world may be drawn back from these
lower planes to another incarnation on earth. On earth the drive
to develop spiritually when not repressed is said to be as intrinsic
as the drive to develop physically, and reincarnation thus provides
a renewed opportunity to learn not to deny this drive in favour of
selfish and material pursuits.

In the afterlife, progress through the planes is said to be more
rapid for spiritually advanced souls, some of whom even pass to the
higher planes immediately after death, bypassing the lower levels
altogether. Johannes Belethus, a 12th-century divine, put it that:

There are many perfect souls which, as soon as they pass from their bodies, flee up into heaven; there are some that are utterly evil who go down to hell; and there are some in the middle between these two ways.

(Shinners 2007)

Experiences in the Plane of Colour

After the Plane of Illusion, the spirit progresses to the Plane of Colour. The transition between the two planes seems to be gradual rather than abrupt, and individuals may only be aware it has taken place when they realize that they now find themselves in increasingly beautiful and harmonious surroundings. It seems from communications that there may even be some interaction between the Plane of Colour and the Plane of Illusion, with souls in the former visiting the latter in order to share their growing wisdom, and since the Plane of Colour is still a realm of illusion it is sometimes difficult to know to which of the two planes a communicator belongs. However, the Plane of Colour (sometimes referred to as the 'Upper Astral' or as 'Summerland' or even as the 'First Heaven') is described as a place of enchanting loveliness, in contrast to the Plane of Illusion which has varied and sometimes starkly contrasting 'landscapes' dependent upon the thoughts and inclinations of the groups of souls responsible for the illusions.

By virtue of its beauty and harmony the Plane of Colour may in fact be the so-called 'paradise' conditions sometimes glimpsed in NDEs. In some NDE reports there are references to a 'beautiful bright light' that is said not to hurt the eyes, and to colours more beautiful than those on earth, while communicators also speak of exquisite flowers and trees and animals. The Rev. Drayton Thomas, a leading member of the SPR in the years before the Second World War and one of the most assiduous of researchers into survival, was informed by his deceased father through leading medium Gladys Leonard that:

...[the] world that is hidden from you is revealed to us, the eye of the soul beholds that which the physical eye cannot see. Now as we go on ... we increasingly perceive the hidden beauty, love and hope in all things. It is not so hidden from us as it is from you. Etta [Drayton Thomas' deceased sister] and I are in a marvellous world.

(Thomas 1936)

He goes on to tell Drayton Thomas that 'scenery' is not only experienced visually, it conveys a profound and direct sense of 'love and hope'. Some communicators describe this as filling them with great bliss, seemingly because they are now closer to the unconditional love that mystics experience as emanating from ultimate reality. W T Stead, a leading psychical researcher and crusading journalist who perished on the *Titanic*, communicated that our own world is an imperfect copy of the reality that he experienced apparently in the Plane of Colour. For example he tells us:

This world which I have been in a long time now, is the closest thing imaginable to your earth ... You will say 'Oh, then it is only a reflection of our world'. It is not that way – the earth is only a reflection of this world. Earth is not the lasting world. It is the training school.

(Stead and Woodman 1922)

However, as communicators insist that the Plane of Colour is not the most exalted level of the afterlife, this suggests that in its turn it is an imperfect reflection of higher states of reality that approximate more closely to the ultimate source of all being. Nevertheless it is the level that features most extensively in descriptions of the afterlife, perhaps because of its apparent similarity to a perfect version of our own world. There is no shortage of such descriptions, and they come not only from scholars and psychical researchers such as Stead and Drayton Thomas' father, but from those who have lived simple yet decent and productive lives. Drayton Thomas' gardener Tomblin, to whom Thomas had occasionally told a little 'of the messages received from ... the Beyond', also proved able to communicate with him after death through Gladys Leonard. The entranced medium, after first supplying a correct description of Tomblin in words that Thomas found 'strongly reminiscent' of the man himself, was then taken over by Tomblin, whose first thought was to thank Thomas for helping him prepare for the afterlife:

> ... I am very pleased you took the trouble to let us know about these things, else I think I should have been real puzzled when I first came over here. I do not think I should have known where I was ... you told us bits and pieces while you talked about other things ... I wish I had followed it up a bit more ... But circumstances do not help us all to go into these things as deep as we ought to do ...

Then, after giving accurate details of his work while on earth and of his family, he went on to say that after 'waking' (presumably in the Plane of Colour, having made the transition directly there from Hades without spending time in the Plane of Illusion):

> I am really thankful; I have a nice little home, a wife [who had pre-deceased him] and garden and many people I am fond of. I'm thankful and content from the bottom of my heart. I shall be often in [your] garden; they will not know I am there, but you will. So I shall find pleasure in seeing things ... The house they had got for me was a really nice cottage ... like a light stone cottage ... they took me out and showed me round. It was just like being on earth, only beautiful weather, sunshine, everything looked splendid and just at its best ...

Tomblin, whom Thomas describes as having been 'a man of quiet thoughtfulness ... of exemplary character and sterling qualities ... [whose] intelligence far exceeded his education', appears from this to be effectively living an idealized extension of his earthly life, with his wife and his house and his garden. This may seem a description of life in the Plane of Illusion rather than in the Plane of Colour, but Tomblin's experiences are consistent with his solid grounding in the natural world and in the life of a gardener. His experiences of the Plane of Colour are exactly suited to his modest, honest way of being and to his sense of the ideal life, a sense that varies from individual to individual. As a man of outstanding qualities with few opportunities to better himself educationally while on earth he demonstrates that entry to the Plane of Colour has nothing to do with wealth or social status or academic achievement, and everything to do with the quality of the soul itself. It is to illustrate this point – particularly as Tomblin's communications were received by a medium with the high reputation of Gladys Leonard and in the presence of a psychical researcher as experienced as Drayton Thomas – that it is so revealing to quote from Tomblin's account.

This account, together with the other examples given a little later, also bears witness to the continuing existence in the Plane of Colour of both a quasi-physical environment and a quasi-physical body complete with quasi-physical senses. A sceptic might argue that this suggests Tomblin's account is an unconscious fabrication by the medium of what she knew Thomas would like to hear, or is the result of telepathic impressions she picked up from Thomas' own wishful thinking or from that of others who knew Tomblin well in life. But Gladys Leonard's long and successful career in mediumship renders it unlikely she would be prone to fabrication, unconscious or otherwise, and the second possibility (known as the 'SuperESP' theory and based on the argument that all mediumistic information comes via telepathy or clairvoyance from this world rather than from the deceased) involves so many debateable assumptions and suppositions as to put it outside the bounds of serious credibility (this point is fully discussed in Fontana 2005 and elsewhere).

In a subsequent sitting with Gladys Leonard, Tomblin gave Drayton Thomas more extensive details of his afterlife experiences.

> ... The first thing I was pleased about was that I should have books and be able to enjoy them ... years ago I had a natural liking for books, and if things had been different with me I might have been rather a scholar ...

A little further on he even tells us of starting to study with a college professor, and of giving the professor in return some help with his gardening.

> ... I told him how anxious I was to be educated, so that I could understand more. I am in his class now ... what struck me most over here is the opportunities ... More opportunities for improving my mind, for understanding what is beautiful, meeting people and talking to them ... I am enjoying every minute.

No-one would begrudge Tomblin the opportunity to make up for lost time by studying books and joining classes under a university professor, but perhaps some might argue that it all still sounds too good to be true. Nevertheless, nothing should be dismissed just because it *sounds* too good to be true. Even things that sound too good to *be* true may nevertheless be true. If Tomblin has a body and a mind, much as he had on earth, then the fact that he retains his memories and his interests and enthusiasms, and that he lives in a world of cottages, gardens and professors and is capable of learning new things and joining a 'class' as he would on earth, is consistent with what we have said so far about the afterlife being a mental world. The Plane of Colour, like the Plane of Illusion, seems to be created in part by the thoughts, expectations and hopes of the souls who reach there, and given that these souls are advanced spiritually and in harmony with each other, and high in spiritual qualities such as peace, wisdom, beauty, love and unselfishness, then we would expect that the environment in which they live would reflect the rarefied nature of their thinking. Tomblin's world is only too good to be true if one believes that humankind is incapable of realizing its loftier ideals.

The beauty of the Plane of Colour

An emphasis upon the beauty of the Plane of Colour is apparent in many other communications. Jane Sherwood's communicator, who we mentioned in Chapter 6 in connection with Hades experiences and who like Tomblin may have bypassed the Plane of Illusion, speaks of a post-Hades '... stabilization of the new body and a growing awareness of a real world again; light, clear outlines and real people moving about in a glorious world'. Elsewhere he speaks of the existence of 'Gleaming palaces and temples and beautiful cities built in elaborate form in surroundings of sur-passing loveliness ... They satisfy the artistic and creative among us, so have a legitimate place in life after all', although he himself prefers to live 'independent of elaborate details'. Astor, Geraldine Cummins' chief communicator, when speaking of the deceased Professor Verrall (who we met in Chapter 6), tells us that he lives near 'an ancient Greek temple and near it an amphitheatre, mountains, sparkling sea and deep blue skies' and goes on to say that '... in his study on earth he used to visualize this scene so often that it has been easy for him to make a reality of it here'.

Reginald Lester's deceased wife also seems to have been drawn towards – or to have helped create – an idealized version of the scenery she loved on earth (Lester 1952). Lester, a prominent London journalist who began investigating mediumship after the tragic death of his wife, was fortunate in having sittings with some of the best-known mediums of his day such as Nan Mackenzie, Estelle Roberts and Elsie Hardwick. During his sittings he not only received detailed information from his wife that the mediums could not have known, and that in his view could not be explained by telepathy from his own mind, but many descriptions of the afterlife. For example, through the entranced Elsie Hardwick, his wife told him:

> Conditions are not very much different from on earth … only far more beautiful. We've got hills and valleys, rivers and sea, trees, flowers, grass – all those things, but so much lovelier. Much of the scenery is not unlike our dear Devon … You haven't got rid of that quaint idea that I'm sort of floating about in space. I'm not doing anything of the kind … It's you who are the shadowy one in comparison! We've got our houses, churches, schools and so on … I have here a complete replica of our home; every bit of furniture just the same … even to the ornaments on the mantelpiece.

The communication also contained the information that some of the people in her world had been 'sleeping for a long while' (presumably resting in what we have described as Hades conditions) before their arrival, and added that 'it all depends how they are when they come over – I mean, what their earth life has been like', which again seems to fit with the possibility that some souls may proceed directly from Hades conditions to the Plane of Colour.

A similar discovery of the home he left behind on earth was reported by the deceased Monsignor Robert Benson, a dignitary in the Roman Catholic Church and the son of former Archbishop of Canterbury Edward White Benson. While on earth Monsignor Benson published *The Necromancers*, a book expressing reservations about attempts to contact the dead, but when communicating through the mediumship of his old friend

Anthony Borgia he apparently took a different view after death. In the course of his descriptions of the afterlife he reported that:

> ... when I was first introduced to my spirit home I observed that it was the same as my earth home, but with a difference. As I entered the door-way I saw at once the several changes that had been brought about. These changes were mostly of a structural nature ... of the description I always wished I could have carried out to my earthly home, but which for architectural and other reasons I could never have done.

Helen Salter (who we mentioned in Chapter 6) when communicating through Geraldine Cummins, spoke of finding herself 'back to childhood and girlhood', and that her deceased parents 'appeared to me as I remember them in the earlier years of my life'.

> They brought with them my very old-fashioned home of long ago and its dear, comfortable ugliness, its books, its papers and its flowers, even the photographs that figured in numbers in Victorian sitting rooms, drawing rooms, studies. How I am enjoying it ... imbued as it is with the fragrance of many memories.
>
> (Cummins 1935)

Thus we are told that there were changes to Monsignor Benson's house as if in response to his earthly wishes, and that Helen Salter found herself in her parents' home of long ago, 'enfolded' in the clutter that was a feature of their lives as Cambridge academics. The idea that others may have created a dwelling of some kind for the deceased may seem far-fetched, but we should remember that when referring to his death and to his Father's house Christ promised his disciples that 'I go to prepare a place for you' (John 14:2).

An idealized material world

Everything mimics so clearly the idealized material world that Monsignor Benson and Helen Salter knew on earth that it suggests there may be a strong mental link between the Plane of Colour and our own world. If Tomblin, Benson and Helen Salter, and many others, are correct that they find themselves with homes resembling those they had on earth, it would seem that the thoughts of people when on earth do indeed help determine their afterlife environment even in the Plane of Colour. The late Paul Beard, one of the most careful and perceptive observers of mediumship and of communications relevant to the afterlife, makes this very point.

> At first it may not be particularly easy to accept this idea of a mentally constructed environment [in the afterlife] intimately appropriate to one's inner self. Yet in some ways this parallels earth experience. Take one's earth house. It has been physically constructed to the plans of an architect or merely to those of a speculative builder. It reflects the thought of this designer. In the furnishings ... the ideas and feelings of the occupiers show themselves; in the pictures and in the books, in all the souvenirs that fill it ...
>
> (Beard 1980)

Paul Beard goes on to say that the 'the mental and emotional images' of the house are carried into the afterlife together with 'the subjective moods, memories and desires which made up its atmosphere', and in the afterlife these are all then translated by thought into a copy of the house.

> ... as every account agrees, it will *seem* perfectly solid to its occupiers; but it will not live on, like obstinate bricks and mortar, and will vanish as soon as their use for it vanishes. This is a glimpse, perhaps, of how the *immediate* afterworld reflects its occupiers ...

'Immediate afterworld' refers to the fact that up to and including the Plane of Colour the soul is still in a world dominated by the illusion of form. In Paul Beard's view, it is the failure by critics to realize that communicators are talking about transient 'bricks and mortar' in an illusory world that has been the main reason for the scorn they have directed at descriptions of the afterlife.

> Early discarnate life is not wholly dreamlike but resembles it; like dreams it contains rapidly changing imagery; unlike dreams this imagery sometimes becomes stable and anchored for considerable periods ... again, unlike dreams, the imagery is not created wholly by the dreamer, but also by others to help him ... other persons, essentially free of the dream themselves, may yet choose to step in and share it for a while, in order to help the newcomer ... those who are confined within their after-death dream usually take what is around them to be completely objective. Once they begin to see that it is not so, then they are beginning to be ready to step out of it into a larger world.

However, Paul Beard also quotes a communicator who explains:

> You can't change big things, you can't change the whole scene around you. That is because it is not only your scene, it belongs to lots of other spirits too, but you can change any little thing, when the change won't affect anybody else.

Professor H H Price, formerly Professor of Logic at Oxford University, who examined the philosophical issues associated with survival of death, concluded that as a 'world of thought' shaped and ordered by the mind in which imagination and visualization can directly produce changes in external reality, the concept of an afterlife is acceptable philosophically (Price 1995). Furthermore he accepted that such a world would be a world of diversity. This being so, it means that the beauties of Devon are fine for those who love Devon, just as Tomblin's house and Professor Verrall's Greek temple were fine for the individuals concerned, but not everyone in the Plane of Colour would wish to live in an illusory Devon or a classical Greek landscape. Those with different cultural experiences on earth would go to venues where like-minded souls have 'created' an environment more suited to their tastes. The remark by Jane Sherwood's communicator that he prefers to live 'independent of elaborate details' supports this point.

However, as Paul Beard emphasized, all these thought-created environments are by their nature temporary. Once the soul realizes this it begins to long for the permanent behind the temporary, the real behind the illusory, and once all opportunities for spiritual development in the Plane of Colour have been satisfied, it is ready to move on to the higher non-illusory levels (which Beard refers to as 'the wider world').

Occupations and interests

The idea of the Plane of Colour as a world shaped and ordered by the mind helps answer the question what do people actually *do* when they are there? Communicators insist that opportunities arise in response to their own wishes, enabling them to follow their earthly interests and also to develop new ones. This suggests the quasi-physical body retains the creative skills and abilities it had during its material existence. Reginald Lester's wife, quoted earlier, emphasized the apparent 'reality' of this body, teasing Lester for his 'quaint idea' that she was 'sort of floating about in space', and assuring him that not only was she doing nothing of the kind, it was he who was 'the shadowy one in comparison!' Thus souls may continue to be scientists, musicians, artists and so on, although their interests would be at a level suitable to their relatively advanced spirituality. Since occupations and interests make little sense without stimulation and achievement, one presumes that such things would also still exist. Together with its harmony and beauty, the Plane of Colour also apparently offers scope for originality and invention, all on a much vaster, more cosmic canvas than on earth.

Even though the fruits of this creativity may only be temporary (as indeed they are on earth), the value of the creative act lies not only in its product but in the opportunities for self-development it provides. It is also said by communicators that creative ideas in the arts and sciences are sometimes conveyed from the afterlife to artists and scientists on earth. These ideas are supposedly usually received unconsciously, but some mediums claim they are aware of channelling new compositions from deceased musicians – Rosemary Brown is perhaps the best example, channelling and performing works during her lifetime ostensibly from Listz, Mozart and many others (Brown 1971). Experts are divided as to the quality of these channelled works, but there are those who accept they bear the hallmark of the composers concerned. There are also cases of complete novels written supposedly by the deceased through the automatic writing of mediums such as Pearl Curran (see Litvag 1972). Not only did Curran produce more than ten lengthy historical novels, their quality was such and their period details so accurate that many consider them beyond the scope of her own rather rudimentary education. Certainly it is difficult to accept the sceptical explanation that they were the work of elements of her own unconscious repressed in childhood by her mother's desire that she devote herself to music.

Other mediums have produced presentable works of visual art, sometimes rapidly and in total darkness, supposedly sent by 'spirit' (an accessible example is provided by the work of healer Mathew Manning, who as a boy, and seemingly without artistic ability of his own, produced very passable drawings apparently transmitted by a number of eminent deceased artists – (see Manning 1974). Sadly, despite the quality of some of the best examples (the worst ones are depressingly mediocre) no-one has received a master-piece by these means. If the offerings really are paranormal, some of their finer points may have been lost in transmission; alternatively they may be the work of impostors in the afterlife masquerading as great men and women. Taken as a whole, it seems that even if eminent musicians, painters and writers from the afterlife really are responsible for the works claimed for them, they do not yet show the creative development that one would hope their authors have experienced.

Some communicators claim that they are involved in caring for people who have just made the transition from earth – in some cases presumably descending to Hades conditions to do so – or of looking after those who have died in childhood and who are said to develop into adulthood in the afterlife. Others speak of an interest in learning more about other cultures and ways of life, and of visiting distant lands not only in the Plane of Colour but also in this world. Yet others speak of devoting themselves to learning, and of attending great 'halls of learning'. Disappointingly, they tell us little of what they are 'learning'. Perhaps some further develop the subjects they were studying on earth, or devote themselves to what could be described as cosmic and spiritual truths. On earth we have only a dim apprehension of profound realities that exceed the scope of our understanding, and possibly in the Plane of Colour these realities become more accessible. (When, during our investigations of mediumship, my colleagues and I have pressed communicators for details of these realities we have invariably been told we 'wouldn't understand' them, which is probably true but which does raise sneaking suspicions that they may not yet understand them fully themselves).

As the Plane of Colour is nearer to the source of creation presumably there is less need for the challenges found on earth. The gardener would no longer struggle with weeds or pests or bad weather, and would concentrate instead on form, design and beauty. The musician and the artist and the poet, freed from competition, the jealousies of colleagues, commercial pressures and publishers' deadlines, would be able to devote him or herself to the creative act as a supreme expression of the human spirit. Motivation would not come through egotistical desires for power or fame or authority, but through devotion to the essence of creativity itself.

Time in the afterlife

Another question frequently asked is whether or not time exists in the afterlife. Communicators certainly mention 'time' at each level of the Planes of Form, telling us for example that souls may remain earthbound for hundreds of years or may choose to spend long periods in the Plane of Colour. In my own experiences with the home circles run by mediums, some communicators instruct those present to hold their next sitting at a specified time and date, and punctually turn up at the appointed hour themselves. In addition, the spiritual traditions all use terms relating to time in the afterlife, but what sense does any of this make if at death we leave behind the space-time material universe? And what might existence be like in the afterlife if in reality it exists outside time?

To answer these questions we must change our common-sense notion of what time actually means. We use the term as if it represents something concrete, but in reality 'time' is an abstraction. What we actually *experience* is not 'time' but a constant process of *change*. The position of the earth relative to the sun changes, the seasons change, the days change, our thoughts change, our bodies change, and we invent a concept called 'time' to refer to this process, and for practical purposes take as our yardstick of 'time' the changing position of the earth relative to the sun. We then divide this yardstick into arbitrary units like hours and minutes and invent a device called a clock to keep a record of these units.

However, even though the changes marked by the hands of the

clock proceed at a regular pace, this is not true for our individual perception of time (which seems to 'speed up' for example as we grow older or when we are enjoying ourselves). And physicists tell us that even the changes marked by the clock alter the closer we travel to the speed of light, so that astronauts hurtling at high velocity over vast distances of space would return to earth having physically aged less than their earthbound contemporaries (this scientific reality is intriguingly similar to tales of mortals 'taken by the fairies' for a few days only to find on their return that years have passed and their contemporaries have all grown old).

In the afterlife *change* also happens, but in a very different way from on earth. The concept of 'time' may therefore persist for those in the illusory lower planes, but will have to do with a quite different reality. Since groups of souls in the afterlife ostensibly create their own illusory reality and the changes associated with physical aging no longer occur, change may take place at different rates for each group, and thus each group will live in its own 'time'. This may help explain the difficulties apparently encountered by communicators when they attempt to locate other deceased individuals in response to requests made to them through mediums on earth, or to communicate with those at higher or lower levels to themselves.

For isolated earthbound spirits, who are not part of any consensus reality, 'time' would be an entirely individual, idiosyncratic experience, meaning that although in some cases hauntings have been reported over many years, for the entity responsible the 'time' concerned might be experienced as much briefer, since little or no change would have taken place in their own illusory reality. In effect, the earthbound spirit would be trapped in what might be called a time warp (*see for example* Webster 1989), and live in their own mentally generated picture of how 'their' house looked during their lifetime on earth (which explains why they are sometimes reported as disappearing through a wall where a door used to be). However, spirits existing at higher levels would presumably be well aware of how time is measured on earth, and perfectly able to conform to this time when attempting communication with humans.

During our research with the Scole Group the communicators always stipulated when the next sitting was to be held and if, while resting in the lounge at Scole after our arrival, we forgot to watch the clock, we would be reminded by a loud rap in a remote part of the room that it was time to make our way to the cellar where the séances were held (see Fontana 2005).

Do memories survive?

Any discussion of the afterlife usually returns frequently to the question of what it is that actually survives. We have already discussed the possible survival of a body of some kind, and of the positive qualities that are further developed in the Plane of Colour. Earth memories also would survive if what we are told about the detailed 'life review' is correct. Indeed, without our memories can 'we' be said to survive? Memories play an essential part in giving us our sense of identity. During our earth lives we remember who we are from one day to the next. Each morning we remember we are the person who went to sleep the previous night. We remember our life history, the information we carry in our heads, and vital skills such as language. We remember our family and our friends, and our feelings for them. We remember sights and sounds and how rain and sunlight feel, and we remember our likes and dislikes, and much more besides. If memory fails to survive death, then how much would be left of our individuality?

Professor C D Broad, one of the most important philosophers to have turned his attention to psychical research and the question of survival, insists that only if the 'disembodied personality' remembered experiences that they had had during earthly life could we say that it had 'survived the death of the body in the full sense in which one's waking personality is reinstated after each period of normal sleep'. In quoting Broad, Professor Hornell Hart (1959) emphasizes the same point. Without memory, we would lack the sense of continuity essential if we are to establish a sense of personal identity (Broad returns to the same subject in his *Lectures on Psychical Research*).

The problem is, how could memory survive if memories are stored only in physical brains that cease to exist at death? But *are* memories stored only in our physical brains? Memory is still something of a mystery to science. We do not know how memory, most of which is composed of non-physical thoughts and images, can be stored in the physical cells of the brain. Our memories are not analogous to the memories of computers. Computers are electrical devices that work on the simple principle of whether or not an electric current is flowing or is not flowing in relevant parts of its circuitry. The switching on or off of the current allows the circuitry to signal 'yes' (if the current is flowing) or 'no' (if it is not) in response to each of the myriad possibilities stored on the hard disc or fed in through the software. This principle allows computers to access vast amounts of 'memory' by carrying out 'yes-no' operations in strict accordance with mathematical logic and at lightening speed.

But human memory is more complex than a collection of 'yes/no' responses and, in the light of present know-ledge, cannot satisfactorily be explained in terms of brain electricity or brain chemistry. And unlike computers, human memory can work illogically and divergently as well as logically, throwing up all kinds of associations that prompt new ideas and emotions such as joy, nostalgia, embarrassment, sadness, anger, excitement, fear and so on. It is true that if certain areas of the brain are damaged memories may be lost, but these memories are quite often recovered subsequently, as if they were also stored somewhere else.

I deplore cruel experiments with living animals, but in the days when such experiments were common, leading brain researcher

Karl Lashley discovered that rats trained to respond to lights showed no reduction in the accuracy of their responses when virtually the whole of the motor cortex of their brains was removed. Similar experiments with monkeys that had been taught to open puzzle boxes established that, although removal of most of the motor cortex led to a few weeks of memory loss, the monkeys subsequently proved able to open the puzzle boxes once again, promptly and without having to relearn the skills involved. In other experiments, Lashley found that rats retained previously learnt abilities even when the neural connections between areas of the cerebral cortex were severed and even when the cerebellum itself was removed.

Even when memory loss occurs in humans following brain injury, Lashley concluded that this does not appear to mean that the memories themselves have irretrievably vanished, simply that there is 'greater difficulty in activating the organizing pattern of these memories'. In other words the memories are still there, but cannot be readily accessed. Even when patients are so severely brain-damaged that they are unable to speak or control their physical bodies, Ian Wilson (1988) points out that they have on occasions been 'found to possess fully competent and even exceptional mental powers if some means of communication can be found for them'. His survey of such instances leads him to conclude that mind 'may be something very much more subtle and complex than indicated by mechanistic theories'.

We can go even further than this and suggest that the relatively new science of neuroplasticity supports the conclusion that mental functions, including memory, are not in fact 'hardwired' into particular parts of the brain (*see* Doidge 2007). In addition, areas of the brain can be trained to take over the function usually associated with quite different areas, which may explain how memories lost after brain injury can subsequently be recovered. Other findings seem to suggest that the mind, through practices such as meditation, can actually initiate this brain training (*see*

Begley 2007), thereby producing physical changes in the brain, a discovery that may support the notion that a non-physical mind is indeed distinct from the brain and able to control its activities in significant ways.

Biologist Dr Rupert Sheldrake takes the view that memory is in fact both 'everywhere and nowhere' (*see* Sheldrake 1990). He criticizes the current theory that memory may be stored – in a manner still unknown – in the connections (the *synapses*) between nerve cells, because if it were then the synapses and in fact the whole nervous system would have 'to remain stable [i.e. virtually unchanged] over long periods of time', whereas in fact brain cells are continually dying out. Furthermore, Sheldrake argues that even if memories are stored physically in the brain, there would have to be not only some additional process that recognizes and retrieves individual memories from the memory store when they are required, but *another* process that has a memory for what it is *that needs to be remembered*. In other words, there must be some sort of 'higher order' memory that recognizes what needs to be retrieved before the 'lower order' processes can find and retrieve it.

None of this establishes that memories must therefore be stored in some non-physical dimension outside the brain, but it does indicate that the possibility must be taken very seriously, particularly as reports show that, while out of their bodies during NDEs, individuals still have access to their memories. Not only do they apparently remember their own identities, they identify their environment and remember their family and friends and the work they still want to do on earth. When given the option of returning to their bodies or leaving them permanently they are able to make informed choices based on memory. In the case of OBEs, individuals have similar command over their memories, remembering the layout of their own houses and of the neighbourhood (one of my friends who has regular OBEs follows familiar streets in an attempt to reach a distant park he wishes to visit). Taken together, the evidence suggests that if the consciousness really is outside the body in OBEs and NDEs, memories cannot be solely dependent upon the physical brain.

We can add that communications from the deceased, assuming they are genuine, show that the deceased still possess their memories. They sometimes give their names and a wealth of personal details, including addresses and the names of friends and family. They give facts about their former professions and interests and, in the case of the SPR communicators responsible for the extraordinary series of post-mortem messages known as the cross-correspondences (*see* Saltmarsh 1938), they show a retention of their detailed knowledge of Greek and Latin classical texts. Communicators also appear to remember the views and opinions they held on earth (even to the extent of claiming they now disagree with some of them), and recall not only the circumstances of their own deaths but even experiences from many years ago. The so-called 'life review' may even indicate that they retain their memories for visual images, emotions and their own actions and behaviour.

The hypothesis that memory does exist, in part at least, outside the brain, is known as the *transmission theory*. It suggests that memory is transmitted to the brain rather than stored by it, rather as signals are transmitted to a television set from a studio rather than created by it, and that if some memories are permanently lost after brain injury this may be analogous to the failure of a damaged television set to show pictures even though the appropriate signals are still being sent from the studio.

However, if memories are not stored in the brain where are they stored? An ancient idea associated primarily with Indian Hindu traditions is that they are stored in the so-called *Akashic Records*, supposedly a vast memory bank that exists somewhere and somehow in the spiritual realms, and that contains a record of everything that has ever happened on earth, but frustratingly supporting evidence is only apparent by its absence. Sheldrake's theory of morphogenetic fields may provide a very much more scientific approach. Dr Sheldrake proposes that *morphogenetic fields* are hypothetical 'fields' that store all the data determining the physical and mental characteristics and abilities of each species, and that such fields are as real as other hypothetical fields like electromagnetic 'fields' and gravitational 'fields' postulated to explain invisible connections between objects across space. We may not know what such hypothetical fields actually *are*, but we can measure their effects.

In his various publications (e.g. 1983 and 1988) Sheldrake provides well-researched evidence of the effects of morphogenetic fields, for example demonstrating that when some members of a species have learnt a new ability other members of the same species, even if they have no contact with the learners, master the same ability significantly quicker. It is as if the details involved become stored in the morphogenetic field, making them subsequently more accessible to all members of the species at an unconscious level. If this is correct, then it may be that not only is there a morphogenetic field for each species, there may also be a personal one for each individual that can be unconsciously accessed by him or her during and after life on earth.

But whatever the mechanisms involved, memories do seem to be carried into the afterlife, though some may be discarded once the lessons of earthly life have been learned. Some communicators claim that aspects of the earth life then come to seem like a dream. Even their former names seem unreal to them, mere labels no longer of any relevance. When I asked a deceased aunt of mine, communicating with me via a medium, for her name in order to check her identity I was given the names of her daughter and son-in-law (names unknown to the medium) with whom she had been living for some years prior to her death. It seemed their names rather than her own were the ones she chose to remember. Communicators may also sometimes make several attempts to recall other personal details (though some of the difficulty may be due to the medium's attempts to grasp what is being communicated), and may prefer to focus on the present doings of surviving relatives rather than upon their own past. It is also possible that the deceased may only access earth memories while there are still people on earth with whom these memories are in some way associated. Once the links with earth are no more, earth memories may fade like remote and rather uninteresting dreams.

The survival of animals and plants

Communicators are unanimous in praising the beauty of the Plane of Colour and make frequent reference to the existence of trees and flowers and animals. If these things exist in the Plane of Colour, do they have objective existence or are they illusory forms, created by the group consciousness of those who loved such things on earth? If they are objective, from whence do they come? Do they begin life in the Plane of Colour or arrive there after death?

The clearest answers to these questions, in my personal experience, were provided recently by communications received during experiments with *Instrumental Transcommunication* (ITC), a method developed in the last half of the 20th century for receiving what are claimed to be spirit communications through electronic media such as audio tapes and radios rather than through a medium (*see* e.g. Bander 1972; Cardoso and Fontana 2004, Fontana 2005). When my colleague Dr Cardoso, who was conducting the ITC research concerned, queried the survival of animals and plants with the communicators the answer received was that 'Everything comes to our world' (which by the descriptions given seems to be the Plane of Colour). The implication of this seems to be that our own world serves as the point at which all life takes its objective existence and begins its long spiritual journey.

It is sometimes claimed that animals have no individual consciousness, in the sense that men and women have, unless they have been in long and close relationships with humans, and that after death they return to the amorphous creative potential from which they arose. However, many of those who work with animals insist that each of them shows every sign of personal consciousness from a young age onwards. If this is so, it makes sense to suppose their survival as individuals. An extensive survey of mediumistic communications by Alain Kardec, the inspiration of the thriving Brazilian Spiritist movement, supported the view that animals have 'an intelligence which gives them a certain freedom of action' and 'a principle independent of matter ... that survives their body' (Kardec 1989). There is certainly little doubt that animals have psychic abilities (*see* Sheldrake 1999), which suggests their consciousness can operate outside the constraints of our space-time physical world. Sir Oliver Lodge went even further and insisted that not only do all organic but even all inorganic creations have an 'etherial double', i.e. a 'double' that continues to exist in a supersensible afterlife.

There is also no shortage of reports of recognizable apparitions of deceased animals, and although many of them are anecdotal (*Fate* magazine published a collection in 1996), a number appear carefully observed. The former President of the Scottish SPR, physicist Patricia Robertson, is in no doubt that she saw the apparition of her cat walk across her lounge, in good electric light, soon after its death, an apparition witnessed simultaneously by her daughter. Those who argue (*see* e.g. Fodor, N 1933) that animal apparitions are not proof that individuality and memory survive, overlook the fact that as these apparitions typically appear in their old haunts and to former owners this suggests the persistence of their memories. The notion that they may be 'thought forms' projected by their owners is unconvincing as (save for accounts from Tibetan Buddhism) there is no evidence the earthly human mind can create such elaborate 'thought forms', especially unconsciously and spontaneously.

If animals and plants do survive death, this presumably means that like humans they possess facsimile bodies that leave the physical world at death and continue in the afterlife. However, is this true only for harmless animals and plants or does it apply to the bacteria and viruses responsible for illness and death? And what about animals that prey on one another? If the answer is yes to both these questions does this mean disease and predatory behaviour exist in the afterlife? The only references to disease that I have come across in the literature or in my own research with mediums is to earthly ailments with which some of the deceased still erroneously believe themselves to be afflicted (e.g. Harrison 2008). Other than these fantasy disabilities, disease and injuries seem to be things of the past.

Similarly, I have found no reference to suggest animals still feed on each other or even on plants. This makes sense, since there is no need for physical sustenance in the afterlife or even for competition over territory or sexual supremacy. This being so, all forms of life could therefore live together in peace. Carl Jung was particularly drawn to Isaiah's prophecy (Isaiah 11:6) that 'the wolf shall ... dwell with the lamb, and the leopard shall lie down with the kid; and the calf and the young lion ... and a little child shall lead them', a prophecy that may be true of the afterlife. In the Plane of Colour, greed, selfishness and the love of power will have long been left behind, and it seems possible that all created life can approach the ideal of paradise.

A question sometimes asked is if plants and animals survive, do they too develop spiritually, and if so what is their goal? The obvious answer is that presumably all living forms continue to develop along their own lines of spiritual evolution until ultimately all become part of an all-embracing community of consciousness, to which each makes its unique contribution (a subject to which we return in the next chapter). Thus every species may have a vital role to play in the pattern of existence. The shamanic cultures once prevalent in Siberia to the north, Africa to the south and the Americas to the west recognized this, as did the ancient Egyptians (who even used birds and animals to symbolize the qualities of their gods), and as did the ancient Celtic traditions that covered much of pre-Roman Britain and western Europe. For these cultures all life was conscious, and their legends are replete with 'nature spirits' or 'divas' said to represent the spiritual reality of animals and plants. This suggests they may have possessed an intuitive awareness that these life forms are blessed with a spiritual nature that transcends the physical, different from but not inferior to our own. Even today people who insist their plants benefit from being talked to, assume the existence of some form of plant consciousness.

Communication and travel

Another question asked about the afterlife is how spirits communicate with each other. Are they still imprisoned in the language of their culture, or are they free to exchange ideas with anyone? Evidence from communicators indicates that words are still used. Sitters at physical séances sometimes report being addressed by so-called independent voices, apparently from thin air or through a trumpet, in words heard and understood by all present (we had this experience during the Scole investigation – see Keen at al 1999, Solomon 2006). At sittings with outstanding physical medium Etta Wriedt, sitters from overseas even claimed that the voices conversed with them fluently and correctly in their own languages, none of which was known to the medium (see Usborne Moore 1915, Wydenbruck 1946). At other times sitters are convinced they recognize the voices of deceased relatives and friends, and even their characteristic habits of speech. On the strength of such reports it would seem spirits do not lose their command of language, at least when communicating with those on earth. However, many communicators claim that in the Plane of Colour telepathy (direct mind-to-mind contact) is typically used so that recipients can receive messages in their own languages.

Evidence for the existence of telepathy in our own world has been steadily accumulating since the 1930s and the pioneering work of Professor J B Rhine and his colleagues at Duke University in the USA (two of the best surveys of the evidence concerned are Radin 1997 and 2006). Results under these controlled scientific conditions are rarely dramatic, but are sufficient to place the existence of telepathic abilities well beyond reasonable doubt (critics who doubt this often manifest a disregard that would not be shown towards evidence in other branches of science), and if telepathy is a fact in our world then so it may be in the after-life. Minds are apparently much more attuned to each other in the Plane of Colour than they are on earth, which would obviously facilitate this direct mind-to-mind contact. Communicators inform us however that they do not (or cannot) use telepathy to invade the privacy of those on earth, so presumably the same holds true in the Plane of Colour, although there may be little need there for the 'privacy' that we guard so zealously on earth.

As for travel, communicators tell us that they can 'walk' if they wish, or use the various methods of transport such as cars and trains created by the mental processes used for houses and cities, or they can travel by the power of the mind alone. Presumably the 'power of the mind' might involve thinking of a particular place and willing oneself to arrive there, and one of the communications from F W H Myers through Geraldine Cummins seems to confirm this.

I have to concentrate my thought for what you might call a moment and I can build up a likeness of myself, send that likeness speeding ... to a friend, to one that is in tune with me. Instantly I appear before that friend, though I am remote from him, and my likeness holds speech – in thought remember, not words – with this friend. Yet all the time I control it ... and as soon as the interview is concluded I withdraw the life of my thought from that image of myself and it vanishes.

Myers seems, in fact, to be maintaining that he can be literally in two places at once by projecting a thought-form of himself. He does not tell us whether his consciousness is divided between the two places, although this seems implied. However, he says he can use this method for visiting one 'who is in tune with me', which suggests the method does not work for other individuals. Perhaps in their case travel takes place in person rather than in projection. It would be interesting to know if the same thing is claimed to be true for travelling to a place rather than to a person. Must one be 'in tune with' a place in order to transport one's image there, which means one might go to favourite places in this way but not to places that are unfamiliar?

There are anecdotal accounts of people or objects being apparently 'dematerialized' in one location and 'rematerialized' in another (so-called *transportation* or *teleportation*) even on earth. In the Old Testament the prophets Ezekiel, Elijah and Habakkuk were variously described as having transported, while in the New Testament both St Paul and St Philip are similarly described. In more modern times one of the most amusing (if not most credible) examples of transportation is that of the medium Mrs Agnes Guppy (Agnes Nichols), who on 3 June 1871 was reportedly transported (seemingly against her prior consent and dressed only in her dressing gown and slippers) from her London home to a séance held by mediums Frank Herne and Charles Williams three miles away. The incident was vouched for by all ten sitters present at the Herne/Williams séance and even by a very angry Mrs Guppy herself. Most people dismissed it at the time as a publicity stunt with a perfectly normal explanation, but though if it was a stunt it backfired badly since it helped ridicule the reputation of all the three mediums concerned.

There are seemingly well-attested accounts of the teleportation of celebrated South American medium Carlo Mirabelli on more than one occasion, most notably over a distance of 90 kilometres from Sao Paulo to San Vicente in 1930. In a case witnessed and vouched for by famed Italian researcher Ernesto Bozzano, Marquis Centurione Scotto was reported to have been transported from a locked room in Millesimo Castle to a granary in the stable yard (for short summaries of these and other cases *see* e.g. Fodor 1933).

There is rather better evidence for the teleportation of inanimate objects and of plants (known collectively as *apports*) in our physical world than there is of humans. I have been present at séances and poltergeist hauntings when coins, keys, stones, small rocks, and other objects have fallen inexplicably from the ceiling sometimes in broad daylight under conditions that rendered fraud extremely unlikely. In the history of psychical research, scientists of the calibre of criminal anthropologist Professor Cesar Lombroso, astronomer Camille Flammarion, physicist Professor Johann Zollner, and psychologist Dr Julien Ochorowitz have all testified to having witnessed the arrival of apports in ways that defied normal explanation. The medium Madame d'Esperance is reported as frequently facilitating the receipt of apports of flowers, some with thorns that would have made it difficult to hide them on her person. Mrs Guppy, she of the supposed teleportation across London, was also well known for apports of flowers both in and out of season. Minnie Harrison was credited with many flower apports, apparently plucked from neighbouring gardens while she was deeply entranced within her circle and the house secured against accomplices or intruders.

We still await the conclusive proof of the existence of apports, such as their arrival in specially constructed tamper-proof locked boxes, but it must be said that the weight of evidence for them is relatively impressive. Quite how we can square their existence with the known laws of physics is another matter, but the possibility that such things happen on this earth makes it a little more credible that they may happen in the afterlife.

Dreams give us some idea of what 'teleportation' might be like, should it occur in the afterlife. In so-called 'lucid dreams' (dreams in which we know we are dreaming and can take control of what happens) we can 'will' ourselves from one place to another. Many of us will also have found ourselves changing locations instantaneously in the dream world. These dream experiences are particularly interesting because, despite the fact that the mind has no reason in waking life to accept such things are feasible, the dreaming mind accepts them as perfectly natural. In OBEs individuals also frequently report finding themselves 'drifting' over the ground without any form of locomotion, or being drawn through the air at great speed by some unknown force (I have personally had both these experiences). Why should the dreaming mind or the mind in an OBE accept such things so readily? If nothing else it shows the power of the mind to create its own reality – a reality moreover that is at dramatic variance with physical reality. If communicators are to be believed, it is this power, unfettered by the constraints of material existence, that is responsible for many afterlife experiences.

Rain or shine?

Those who live in a climate as fickle as that in Britain may wonder if they would have to put up with something similar in the afterlife. If communicators are to be believed it seems there is little reason to worry, at least for those reaching the Plane of Colour. Communicators refer to a bright light that, unlike the sun, 'does not hurt the eyes' and that illuminates a beautiful blue sky. There is no mention of rain or cold, only of a balmy pastoral climate. Darkness does seem possible, however, for those who wish to 'sleep' – presumably a 'sleep' that facilitates certain forms of learning. It all sounds very comfortable, and perhaps we are due some comfort after the vicissitudes of the physical world. Communicators also tell us of the much greater freedoms experienced in the Plane of Colour. Even the pleasures of swimming are seemingly available, in water said to be deliciously warm and refreshing and without the need to struggle with damp towels and unco-operative clothing afterwards. Like trees, flowers and all life, water is said to be far more beautiful than on earth, pure and clear and sparkling under the bright blue of the sky. It seems that increasingly one is able to touch the glory of life itself, of the beauty and lightness of being.

On earth this glory is obscured by all manner of physical and psychological concerns so that for much of the time we are unable to savour the sheer joy that the gift of life brings. We rarely glimpse the beauties of the world of form in all its essential harmony and peace, or experience relationships that are free from the stress of anxieties and jealousies and the fear of loss. If the reports of com-municators are correct, the Plane of Colour is this world made perfect, the archetypal, ideal world of which the earth is a very imperfect copy. It is in fact the ultimate manifestation of form, the pure expression of what is possible when perfect harmony reigns between all beings.

Having been enriched and transformed by such an ideal world, and drawn closer through the experiences it offers to the source of all being, why would one eventually wish to move on? There may be many reasons, but even in our present world we have an innate longing to learn more, to strive for something beyond our grasp, to travel beyond the next bend in the road or beyond the crest of the next hill. In the Plane of Colour this longing may take an essen-tially spiritual form, a desire to draw ever closer to the source, and eventually this longing may take individuals to the next level in their journey. From what we are told of the Plane of Colour it does not, for all its formal perfection, provide the seeker with all the answers to the meaning and purpose of life. And is there, at some point, the hope of the vision of the Divine to which the religious mind aspires?

Moving on

We are told that eventually all individuals develop to the point where they move on to the next plane (except for those very rare occasions when communicators tell us that even from this level some individuals may choose reincarnation on earth). What form might this development take? During the Scole investigation the communicators indicated that one of their practices is to go on retreats, and sometimes one or other of our communicators would be absent for many sittings for this purpose. The communicators also spoke of learning from beings at higher levels than themselves, and often they transmitted messages to us from these beings who were said to be no longer able to communicate readily with earth. There was also talk by communicators of a second, much more lengthy and detailed life review than the one that occurs soon after death. This review enables the individual to build upon the work done in the first review, and to learn more profound lessons from the mistakes made on earth, and to empathize more fully with those who may have been harmed in any way by these mistakes. Distressing feelings of guilt and remorse were fully experienced and laid to rest in the first review and during the experiences at the lower planes, and the emphasis is now upon fully developing the potential shared by all men and women for love and understanding, and for extending forgiveness to those by whom one may have been harmed while on earth. All hatred, resentment, bitterness, jealousy and other destructive emotions are now finally put aside, and the spirit at last allowed to become free from the burdens that they represent, and to abide at last in its own true nature.

In a sense, this is the final stage in the death of the negative aspects of the old self. For this reason the Plane of Colour is sometimes referred to as the Plane of Emotional Harmony, the plane where the wellspring that drives emotional energy exists in its pure life-enhancing essence before it becomes fragmented by individual human and animal consciousness on earth. In this emotional harmony there is no strife, no discord, only perfect love and the unimaginable bliss and peace that accompany perfect love.

If communicators are to be believed, the second life review also enables the individual to recognize all the opportunities for inner development and for offering love that were given to him or her and not taken on earth. Christians emphasize that these and other failures arise from our refusal to live life in accordance with God's law as revealed in Christ, while Hindus stress they are due to our inability to recognize our fundamental unity with Brahman (the Absolute). But implicit in all the great spiritual traditions is the belief that our failures involve a basic refusal to direct our lives towards a higher purpose than self-gratification and attachment to the transitory pleasures of the material world. Why should we have to learn this from our experiences instead of being created with the necessary knowledge already in place? The answer seems to be that this is in fact *the process* of our being created with the necessary knowledge. This process is happening now and in the afterlife, rather than having occurred before birth. As humans we are indeed a work in progress rather than in any sense the complete article, and this is simply the way things are.

Chapter Ten

·

THE FORMLESS REALMS

A major departure

The Plane of Colour seems to represent an end to sickness and suffering, a place where the power of thought replaces physical effort and where peace and love rule; and where one can follow chosen interests without the fear of failure or the stress of competition in the company of like-minded friends. In addition, the Plane of Colour is attained only after lengthy and demanding spiritual development on earth and in the initial levels of the afterlife. What could be more heavenly? Can there be higher realms than this? We are told that there are, and that these are the three 'formless realms'. But even if this is true, why would anyone want to ascend to these levels? Why not remain in the Plane of Colour?

This question was partially answered at the end of the last chapter, but now we can go further and say that the formless planes mark a major departure from the four lower realms in that they are said to be no longer illusory but to approach successively closer to an ultimate reality in which consciousness is not limited by the need to accommodate to a physical body and to time and space, whether actual or illusory. Esoteric Christian traditions even equate the first of the formless planes, the so-called Plane of

Flame, with the Holy Spirit, the second of them, the Plane of Pure Light, with Christ, and the highest plane of all, the Seventh Heaven, with God the Father. Thus the three formless realms are seen collectively as the sphere of the Holy Trinity.

Both Hinduism and Buddhism also lay particular stress upon the formless realms. One way of thinking about what they might represent, when compared to the realms of form, is to ponder the question posed by Lama Govinda, an outstanding Buddhist teacher (Govinda 1977), namely do we identify with 'the infinite and imperishable or with the finite and ephemeral?'. Are we ephemeral beings limited by form, or infinite beings unlimited by the constraints of our own illusions? The human spirit has an imaginative awareness of infinite possibilities, of something greater and nobler than its own limited self, a spiritual longing to rediscover the source from which it arose. What in fact is the goal of our journey, the ultimate purpose and meaning of our exist-ence? The materialist is convinced there is none, but throughout history many (at times probably the majority) of men and women have sensed the reality of the ineffable, a sense that arises from direct mystical experience rather than from hearsay or speculation.

Within all the great spiritual traditions there are teachings referring to higher states that enable the individual consciousness to draw nearer to the ultimate reality of which it is a part. Mystics in all the great traditions have touched these states, if only briefly. Their experiences are difficult to put into words, since by their nature they lie effectively beyond language, but the similarities between the descriptions we have of mystical visions from all the great traditions indicate that they each refer to the same awareness of what lies beyond the realms of illusion, of which the Plane of Colour, for all its formal beauty and perfection, remains a part.

A feature of the descriptions of the four realms of form is that, albeit in progressively rarefied versions, they are worlds of objects, of things. Essentially even the Plane of Colour is an idealized version of our present world, stripped of its problems and challenges and disadvantages. And although the realms of form are realms in which increasingly the challenges of existence are presented not by the environment but by self-examination, and in which learning has less to do with the outer world and more to do with the inner one, they are still worlds in which form is imposed upon reality. Like a veil, the illusion of form comes between human consciousness and the true essence of being. For all its beauty, form is a product of this essence rather than the essence itself. In the Plane of Colour the soul is still enclosed in form, separating it from other souls and fragmenting the spectrum of reality. Thus, despite its great attractions, the Plane of Colour is still an aspect of the finite and ephemeral rather than an expression of the infinite and imperishable, and therefore ultimately unsatisfactory.

The realms of form, particularly the earth plane, are said by all the great traditions to offer experiences from which we can learn progressively deeper and deeper lessons. Which raises again the question posed at the end of the last chapter, 'why should all this learning be necessary – why can't we be created perfect, with no lessons needed?' As before, the answer is that learning would seem to be part of the process of creation. We can see from nature that creation is not a once-and-for-all event. The seed grows into the seedling, the seedling grows into the tree and so on, just as the baby grows into the child and the child grows into the adult. Creation is gradual rather than instant. The act of creation is not confined to conception or to birth or to physical life, but is an enduring process that continues into the afterlife. For those who then want to know why does creation have to be gradual, why does a process have to be involved, I can best offer the answer given to my brother and myself when we put this very question to an eminent Hindu teacher, 'Go and find God and ask him' (words whose deeper significance has become increasingly apparent to me as time has gone by). It is simply the way that creation is. We are each an expression of the infinite diversity of reality, and we should be grateful that we are given our own particular part to play in the universal scheme of things. We are, as I said in the last chapter, a work in progress rather than the finished article.

The 'second death'

Once the learning process that begins on earth and culminates in the Plane of Colour is complete, the individual is ready to move on. As the Plane of Colour is changeable by thought and by desire, the soul comes to see that it is not only illusory but transitory and impermanent, and therefore cannot be the infinite and imperishable reality to which the soul aspires. Rather it is a transition between the world of form, to which we have become accustomed on earth and which has now fulfilled its purpose, and the formless realms that lead closer to the source of our existence. It has shown the soul the ultimate perfection of form and allowed it to recognize, in its own time, that even this perfection is not ultimately sufficient.

We are told by communicators that the transition between the Plane of Colour and the formless planes is more marked than the transition between each of the planes of form, so much so in fact that it is sometimes described as a 'second death' because one is now 'dying' to the illusions that held one captive, and leaving behind the illusory (or astral) body, just as in the first death the physical body was left behind. This 'second death' is said to involve a boundless elevation of consciousness, as one is now able to move closer to the source of this consciousness. The first death occurred when the soul was separated from the physical body at the end of its earthly existence, and now, in a second death, the soul separates itself from the illusory body and the illusory world of form. It is said that the second death is much less traumatic than the first, and is undertaken joyfully and only when the individual decides the time is right.

According to accounts of the second death, the soul settles into a sleep-like state, and like all illusions, that of a body fades gradually away. When the process is complete, the soul awakens in the formless realms which, as they are nearer the infinite potential from which all things arise, represent an exponential expansion of opportunities. Nothing of value is lost, everything of value is gained.

The formless realms are thus only attained after a gradual process of recognizing the illusory and ultimately unsatisfactory nature of form as we experience it, and becoming increasingly conscious of the extraordinary nature of what lies beyond and behind form. In the formless realms it is not that one has turned one's back on form, but that one is no longer limited by it. One is free to experience the source from which all that is beautiful and inspiring about form arises. Imagine the most beautiful and life-enhancing Greek statue known to you. Now focus on the ideal of perfection, the essence of beauty, of which the statue was thought by the Greeks to be merely an imperfect copy. Now summon up the idea of the infinite potential from which the essence itself arose, formless in that it contained the essence of all forms.

Universal truths

From the ancient Greeks onwards (and perhaps from even earlier times) it has been explained by theologians and certain philosophers such as Aquinas and Plato that this many-sided 'essence' is the source of absolute, eternal and universal truths or standards, not only of beauty but of goodness, purity, love, truth and peace, revealed by the gods or by God and from which humankind gains its concepts of right and wrong. Why should we accept this explanation? One answer is that the alternatives proposed by materialist philosophers as to the origin of concepts of right and wrong are neither absolute nor universal, nor are they eternal. Such alternatives can broadly be reduced to three belief systems, namely that humankind is governed simply by what is (i) expedient for the individual (the view taken by the Sophists); or (ii) by what is perceived to be the greatest good of the greatest number (the view taken by the Utilitarians); or (iii) by an evolutionary process that favours the survival of those best suited to survive (the view taken by the neo-Darwinians). Under any of these systems one could justify euthanasia for those considered non-productive members of society, cannibalism in times of famine, and compulsory sterilization for individuals deemed socially undesirable. The human race has many failings, but mercifully we have some essential sense of right and wrong that leads us to recoil from such barbarity.

Consequently, we may prefer the explanation of absolute and eternal standards. Philo Judaeus, the 1st-century Hellenistic-Judaic philosopher whose writings greatly influenced Greek-Christian theologians, labelled these standards *archetypes* and also used the term to stand for the *imago Dei*, the God-image accessible to man (Carl Jung employed the term more widely to stand for the 'universal images that ... make up the contents of the collective unconscious'). These standards or qualities are thought of as formless (hence the need to represent them in symbolic form) but to have an existence far more real than anything that characterizes the transitory worlds of form. Philo Judaeus maintained that they provide the basis for much of the soul's identity, and are what endures when the soul has been progressively purified of its selfish and egotistical desires. Increasingly the soul is therefore able to recognize its unity with other souls, though this does not necessarily imply the loss of individuality which may have its own archetypal purpose, as we discuss in due course. However, gender is no longer a divisive issue, as masculine and feminine archetypes exist equally within each soul.

It may seem odd to have to go back to a 1st-century Greek philosopher and his followers for possible insights into the formless realms, but it only appears odd because we think ourselves so much wiser than men and women who lived 2,000 years ago. This modern arrogance and its belief in eternal progress would be amusing if it were not ultimately so destructive. Universal eternal standards were as accessible in the early centuries CE to the ancient Greeks as they are to us today.

Experiencing formlessness

In the formless realms, it is said that the soul approaches closer to a full experience of these archetypes. But what might formlessness itself be *like* for those who achieve the formless realms? When Buddhism talks of 'formless realms' the term seems to refer to realms in which phenomena are 'empty of independent, concrete existence' (or of 'selfhood' as it is sometimes called), which implies for some people that it means an end to independence and individuality (*see* Dalai Lama 2000).

Ian Wallace, one of the leading interpreters of Buddhism to the West, speaks of the formless realms as 'a purely abstract domain of reality', and to some this also suggests a mindless vacuum, equivalent to annihilation, but obviously this is not what is intended. If it were, there would be no point in wasting time talking about it since formlessness would simply be another word for extinction and the end of everything. Buddhism is at pains to make clear it is no such thing, describing it for example as an 'infinite, radiant empty awareness' (*see* Wallace 2007).

Tibetan Buddhism divides human faculties into five groups of what it calls 'aggregates', namely the aggregates of the body, of the feelings, of discrimination, of compositional factors and of consciousness. In the formless realms it tells us that:

> Beings ... have only four aggregates; they lack the form aggregate. Thus, they have no external form.
>
> (Lati Rinpochay et al 1983)

If this is so, inner experience continues in a recognizable way to retain feelings, discrimination, compositional factors and consciousness, but to be free from the self-centredness and the physical desires, demands and limitations associated with the body that govern so much of our behaviour while limited by form. Freed from such accretions, the four aggregates can manifest in their essential purity of wisdom and love.

From a Christian standpoint, St Irenaeus puts it that:

Neither the structure nor the substance of creation is destroyed.
It is only the outward form of this world that passes away.

It is claimed that in deep meditation one can experience something of this formlessness as awareness of the physical body and of the external world of physical objects and events falling away, and one abides in pure consciousness itself, a reality much more real than anything experienced through the bodily senses. These senses provide us with only an indirect experience, an interpretation of existence, while pure consciousness is existence itself. It is said that as the physical senses are transcended so is the illusory 'desire realm' to which these senses relate. In meditation, as the 4th-century Christian St Basil tells us, the 'mind returns to itself, and by means of itself ascends to the thought of God', while St Isaac in the same century tells us to 'Enter eagerly into the treasure house that is within you ... dive within yourself, and in your soul you will find the stairs by which to ascend' (see Ware 1979).

Normally the external world so dominates consciousness that we rarely turn our attention to this deep internal state of whose existence we may in fact remain unaware for a whole lifetime. Denma Locho Rinboche, a leading Tibetan scholar and meditation master, puts it that:

The meditator does not take to mind any external phenomena, even space, but only his or her own mind. Space is an external phenomenon that is not included in the mental continuum. Thus the object is one's own consciousness.

(Lati Rinbochay et al 1983)

Elsewhere the same writer tells us that this state of 'pure consciousness' is not only blissful but is 'actual bliss', far superior to what we refer to as 'bliss' in ordinary life. Hindu traditions also speak of this rarefied level of 'bliss', which along with 'being' and 'consciousness' is said in fact to be one of the attributes of Brahman, the Supreme Absolute, from whom all creation arises. Thus Hindu thought teaches that when experiencing this pure consciousness the meditator is experiencing an aspect of the mind of Brahman. These are deep matters, too complex to pursue in detail here, but they are touched on because they indicate that 'formlessness' is not a theoretical concept associated only with the afterlife but a living reality that the committed and accomplished meditator can taste while still in the here and now.

Music is perhaps another way of obtaining a hint of what 'formlessness' might mean, which may be why music is so frequently mentioned as present in the heavenly realms. Music can be said to have a structural 'form', and it also creates sound waves that can be recorded and measured, but neither the structure nor the recording and measurement are what music actually is. For the listener, the music is not experienced as structure or as sound waves but as music. Not surprisingly music has always been regarded as akin to magic, and there does appear to be something supernatural about its ability to alter the consciousness of the listener. It can arouse deep emotions, evoke memories, create associations and, at its most profound, inspire transcendental states similar to those experienced in deep meditation. Music can take us into a formless inner realm beyond words and concepts – something that even the rather trite remark that music 'takes us out of ourselves' seems to recognize.

However, if the aggregates of the body are laid aside, how is it that during NDEs some individuals report not only seeing a beautiful light but also seeing 'Beings of Light' whom they identify with angels or with Christ or (in the case of individuals from other religious tradition) with gods or bodhisattvas? Assuming that these 'Beings of Light' are from the formless realms, how can they be seen as forms when they have passed beyond the realms of form? The answer is that nowhere are we told that attaining the formless realms means the soul cannot assume a 'form' again for the benefit of those at lower levels of spiritual development. Free now from the constraints both of form and of the illusions of form, it can appear in whatever idealized appearance is most helpful to the spiritual understanding of the observer. As the soul journeys through the various levels of the afterlife the range of possibilities open to it progressively increase.

The Plane of Pure Flame

The Plane of Pure Flame is the first of the formless realms, and the first plane at which the limited self is transcended and the soul thus realizes freedom from the limitations of space and time, of here and there, of objects and things. A Hindu description sometimes refers to this as the 'dewdrop slipping into the shining sea', but a Zen Buddhist abbot once told me that he preferred the description that 'the dewdrop *becomes* the shining sea'. Whichever metaphor we prefer, it should not be taken to imply that the soul merges with some amorphous unity and thus loses any sense of individual existence. Rather the metaphors point to the fact that the soul passes beyond narrow descriptions like unity and individuality, beyond the restriction of opposites and the tyranny of 'either-or', and realizes for the first time what it has always been.

Tibetan Buddhism recognizes the existence of 28 divine realms (18 of which are said to be realms of 'desireless form', and only 4 realms of pure formlessness), but it would take a book twice as long as this to even touch the complexity of the concepts involved, and the realm known by Tibetan Buddhism as the *Devachan* (the 'Dwelling of the Shining Ones') seems to be the realm most analogous to the Plane of Flame. However, Buddhism teaches that even from the Devachan, rebirth on earth is inevitable. Often referred to as 'Heaven' or the plane of the gods, the Devachan is attained by those who have gained exceptional merit in their earthly lives, but (in a rather subtle piece of logic) it is claimed they have still not achieved final enlightenment as they become 'attached' to the blissful happiness of the Devachan. Accordingly, once their store of merit is exhausted, they must be reborn on earth, the only place where final enlightenment is possible.

One possible way of explaining the contrast between the continuing Buddhist emphasis upon rebirth and the Western belief that even if rebirth is ever possible it certainly does not take place from the higher planes of the afterlife, is that whereas the latter accepts the reality of spiritual progress in the afterlife the former (with the exception of the Pure Land Buddhist tradition which we discuss in due course) appears not to do so. As far as I know there has been no real attempt from East-West dialogues on religious belief to address these differences. But if they were addressed the Western Christian position would be that a new covenant between God and humankind was made manifest in Christ, and that this covenant embraces redemption and forgiveness (hence spiritual progress in the afterlife) for those who accept the reality of this covenant. Thus Christianity teaches the importance of *other* power. Men and women cannot redeem themselves without the gift of Christ's love.

Buddhism on the other hand teaches the importance of *personal* power. Enlightenment and consequent freedom from ignorance and from attachment to the physical world come through the individual's own efforts. He or she can be guided by the teachings of the Buddha and of other sages, but the Buddha always stressed personal power, and his dying words to his disciples were (in translation) reported to be 'Work out your own

salvation with diligence'. Ultimately, the responsibility for salvation (enlightenment in Buddhist terms) rested principally with
them. Thus for the Christian it follows that through the grace of
Christ and a life lived in love and obedience to Christ one does not
return to earth, while to the Buddhist it makes sense that if one has
not completed one's quest for enlightenment one must return to
earth to take up the search once again.

Can we say therefore that at the higher levels Christians and
Buddhists, and perhaps those in other spiritual traditions, may
follow different paths in the afterlife? Perhaps. However, both
Christian mystics and Buddhist mystics describe the mystical
experience in similar terms, as a revelation of universal love and
unity, and both Christianity and Buddhism teach that the path to
this revelation is a way of life based upon compassion, selflessness,
non-violence, morality, forgiveness, and peace, which suggests that
we should not overemphasize the differences at the expense of
missing the similarities. And obviously there are possible pitfalls
in both paths. Christians may feel they can leave it all to Christ
who will forgive their sins even though they may live unchristian
lives, while Buddhists may feel there is no spiritual power beyond
themselves on which they can call for help. Ultimately, in avoiding
these pitfalls, each person makes his or her own choice between
the paths that lie open to them.

In the Plane of Pure Flame the soul would presumably have its
first experience of the archetypes in their pure essence, as opposed
to the confused and diluted way in which they manifest in and
through the world of form. For example, on earth we recognize
beauty in nature, in the human body, in animals, in works of art,
but what we are seeing are representations of beauty as expressed
and limited by our imperfect world, which is very different from
experiencing the archetype of beauty in and of itself. As with
formlessness generally, it is hard to know what experiencing the
archetype or essence of beauty would be 'like', for comparisons
with the facts of normal experience are obviously inadequate.

However, at some profound level we do have a hint of its nature, since if the ideal archetype of beauty exists it is already within us, no matter how heavily it is obscured by our material existence. By virtue of the fact it is within us we recognize beauty when we see it, and by virtue of the fact it is within us artists strive to express it through shapes and colours, enabling their work to inspire others by appealing to a potential that is already there. We can also respond to the insights provided by the mystics and even by ordinary men and women who have had extraordinary experiences (*see* Hay 1987 for relevant examples), and through meditation or through a deep relationship with nature we can even perhaps encounter something of these experiences for ourselves.

Communicators inform us that, once in the formless realms, it becomes increasingly difficult to communicate directly with the lower realms of form, which is apparently why higher souls contact those in the Plane of Colour who then relay the messages concerned to earth, although even the latter reportedly speak of the earthly 'atmosphere' as dense and heavy, as if they are moving through a murky clinging fog. However, those in the Plane of Flame who have a particular mission to impart advanced teachings directly to the earth realm are supposedly able to do so.

The fact that such advanced spirits so often turn out to be Native American or Chinese is a frequent cause for both mirth and scepticism, but the explanation usually given by mediums is that the spiritual traditions of both Native Americans and Chinese (specifically those Chinese who followed the Taoist religion) had a particularly strong spiritual relationship with our natural world. Thus their spiritual practices while on earth enabled them to form an abiding link between spirit and matter, a link that has allowed them to remain in contact with the levels of form even though they themselves are in the Plane of Pure Flame. Like the Beings of Light, who are associated with even higher levels, they are supposedly able to materialize in human form and become briefly visible, at least to clairvoyants. I once saw such a materialization myself in full electric light when sitting with a medium under conditions that excluded trickery. No matter how incredible it may sound, I know what I saw, totally unexpectedly as there was no prior mention of a possible materialization, and my experience was shared with two others also present at the time.

In some traditions the Plane of Pure Flame is referred to as the 'Causal Plane', as it is said to be the point at which the life force commences its passage from formlessness into the realms of form, thus beginning the creative process that reaches completion on earth before commencing its upward ascent back towards the source. It is also said to be the plane of perfect intellectual harmony, the plane where the wellspring that inspires thought and the intellect exists in its pure life-enhancing essence before it becomes fragmented by individual human and animal conscious-ness on earth. In this intellectual harmony there is no strife, no discord, only the expression of the pure archetype of mind itself. The term 'Plane of Pure Flame' symbolizes this intellectual purity, and also symbolizes the fact that, in their total freedom, thought and the intellect can take on any form they please, just as flames are eternally free to change their shape when dancing in the wind.

The Plane of Pure Light

Whereas a flame symbolizes freedom from the restrictions of form, light symbolizes infinity itself. Thus the Plane of Pure Light is said to remove the last limits upon human consciousness, allowing it to access cosmic consciousness, the consciousness of all life and order throughout creation. According to Richard M Bucke (1956), cosmic consciousness, glimpsed sometimes in deep mystical experience even on earth, is a complete realization that the cosmos is a living presence, that life is eternal, and that ultimate reality is founded upon the spirit of love. Meister Eckhart, the great 13/14th-century Christian mystic, when speaking of mystical experiences at this level, put it that 'We feel an inkling of the perfection and stability of eternity, for there is neither time nor space, neither before nor after ...' (*see* Pfeiffer 1924).

Can we equate the Plane of Pure Light with the Kingdom of Heaven of the scriptures? Certainly it seems to reflect the ideals of perfection taught by Christ, and to approach close to the Divine source of all life. Pure, undefiled and the essence of universal love, wisdom and harmony, it approaches in many ways the sublime vision that the Christian entertains of heaven, and in certain traditions of esoteric Christianity it is spoken of as the realm of Christ himself. Buddhism terms it the *Sukhavati* Heaven (the Pure Land or Western Paradise), and the Buddha who is said to 'rule' over it, Buddha Amitabha, is known as the Buddha of *Boundless Light*. According to the teachings of the Pure Land (or *Shin*) school of Mahayana Buddhism, there is no return to earth from the Sukhavati Heaven, entry into which is gained by total devotion to Buddha Amitabha (Japanese Amida) during life on earth (*see* Suzuki 1979).

Amitabha is said to have vowed not to enter nirvana until all beings down to 'the last blade of grass' can enter with him, and by ascending to the Sukhavati plane after death all the individual's 'sins and evil passions' are thus transferred to Amitabha, who has such an inexhaustible store of merit that he can take these upon himself and free the devotee from his bad karma. Pure Land Buddhism accepts that achieving enlightenment while on earth is almost impossibly difficult for the ordinary mortal in this degenerate age, therefore Amitabha has created his Pure Land as a place where the final step to enlightenment can be taken more easily.

Essentially, Pure Land Buddhism (now the largest school of Buddhism in both Japan and China), like Christianity, teaches the importance of *other* power. Amitabha takes on himself the sins of devotees, and effectively grants forgiveness. Suzuki, one of the most influential interpreters of Buddhism for the West, while being alert to the differences, emphasizes this has many similarities with

Christianity, and as Pure Land was founded in 402 CE in China it has been suggested that it may have been influenced by Christianity, which had travelled from North Africa eastwards along the trade routes. Be this as it may, Pure Land rejects what Donran, one of the founders, called 'the hard way' of other Buddhist schools, and fosters the so-called 'easy way' in which one places one's trust in external help. Pure Land teaches that the relationship devotees have with Amitabha during their earth lives will determine whether they enter his kingdom after death, and that entry is direct for devotees who have followed a commitment to perform very many thousands of repetitions of his mantra together with intense visualizations that, performed correctly and with the necessary dedication, cause Amitabha and his Pure Land to arise before the spiritual eye of the practitioner. Many of the ideals of compassion, selflessness and of a developing relationship to ultimate reality are also shared between Christianity and Pure Land.

The Seventh Plane

Above the Plane of Pure Light lies the Seventh Plane, the highest of the seven realms that are said to make up life. At this level, we are told that the soul is now able to enter into 'Contemplation of the Supreme Mind' which could not have happened before as the soul would not have been able to comprehend the experience. The Old Testament warns that man, as ordinary physical man, cannot look upon the face of God – for example we are told that when God speaks to Moses from the burning bush Moses 'hid his face for he was afraid to look upon God' (Exodus 3:6). The Plane of Pure Light introduced the soul to cosmic consciousness and now at last it is able to comprehend at least something of the Supreme Mind, the source from which cosmic consciousness arises.

The Seventh Plane seems equated in some ways with the Tibetan Buddhist *Tushita* Heaven, where the next Buddha,

Maitreya, is said to wait for the appropriate time to be born on earth. Descriptions of the Tushita Heaven (also of the Devachan and the Sukhavati Heavens) are of places of breathtaking beauty, which is rather confusing if they are indeed formless realms, but perhaps this reflects the inadequacy of our language.

Beyond the Tushita Heaven is nirvana, the ineffable, which is said to be beyond all form and formlessness and beyond all conceptualizing. Even the Buddha would not be drawn on descriptions of nirvana, beyond informing his disciples that it is 'unborn, unoriginated, uncreated and unformed' in contrast to our 'born, originated, created and formed' phenomenal world. Nirvana would thus seem to represent a final release from all the limitations of existence. Once one attains nirvana one 'disappears' and there is no return. However, some selfless souls who qualify for entry refuse to do so until all other beings are able to enter with them. Termed *Bodhisattvas*, they are said to return to earth, life-time after life-time, purely to teach and help others. Bodhisattvas have nothing to gain personally since they are already fully enlightened and thus free from the ego and its cravings. No matter what one thinks of the reality of this, it is surely a supreme ideal of selflessness since the Bodhisattva is even beyond the inner rewards such as self-satisfaction that arise from selfless actions.

Descriptions of the Seventh Plane suggest it takes us further into the mystery of pure being, or ultimate reality. Can we say anything about this pure being? Hinduism speaks of it as Brahman, the Absolute, about which nothing can finally be said since any statement about Brahman is automatically incomplete. 'Being, Consciousness and Bliss' – *Sat Chit Ananda* – are the closest the Hindu gets to a description. For Christian mystics such as Eckart it is the Godhead, the supreme absolute reality from which our concepts of God arise (see Forman 1991). Central to these concepts is, of course, the Trinity of God the Father, God the Son and God the Holy Spirit, a Trinity that is both immanent (within us) and transcendent (beyond us). For Christianity, although it might be said that the active principles of Christ and of the Holy Spirit are symbolized in the first two formless realms, nevertheless in their essence they are One with the Father in the Seventh Plane. The Trinity and the Seventh Plane are therefore, for the Christian, the mystery of all mysteries, the alpha and omega of all being, the source of all that we are, all that we have, and all that we may be.

If this is the case, is the Seventh Plane the end of our journey, a return to the source from which we came? And if so what does this 'return', this 'contemplation of the Supreme Mind' actually mean? Advaita Vedanta, one of the three great schools of Hindu thought, teaches that Brahman (the Absolute) and the individual souls of men and women (the Atman) and the whole of manifest creation are in reality One, and that ultimately everything returns to the One (the 'dewdrop slipping into the shining sea').

Dvaita Vedanta, another of the three schools, takes a different view, teaching that as Brahman is consciousness as well as being and bliss, and as consciousness implies the existence of phenomena of which to be conscious, individual souls remain as aspects of this phenomena (and were indeed created for this purpose).

Vishishtadvaita Vedanta, the third of the three Vedantic schools, takes an intermediate position and teaches that the reality of the individual indeed resides fully in the reality of Brahman, but that the individual is also real as an individual and represents divine realities such as truth, beauty and goodness that cannot be reconciled with the impersonal abstraction taught by Advaita.

Buddhism is similar in some ways to Advaita Hinduism, and teaches that those who enter nirvana do not return, but 'disappear' beyond mortal ken. However, although they lose their distinctive personalities, this does not mean they become extinguished, like a flame being blown out. What is blown out is their illusory self, the person they thought they were, the self-created image that they had come to believe was who they really are. As Edward Conze, one of the leading interpreters of Buddhism, put it (after warning us that it is almost impossible to explain) 'they do not all become the same, but retain some separate and distinctive features' (Conze 1967). Individual selfhood is transcended, but an aspect of transcendent reality remains, even as the Buddha himself was an aspect of this reality.

Christianity, while teaching that the soul comes to know God 'face to face', does not teach that it is absorbed into God. As John Hick (1976) puts it, the soul attains to a 'hard-to-define state of both unity and diversity in which there is a merging into one, and yet the many remain somehow many ...'. In more orthodox Christian language, the soul enjoys both the bliss of its true relationship to God as the ground of its being, and of contemplating divine reality. Subjectivity and objectivity are no longer opposites, but expressions of the one fundamental truth.

Sri Ramakrishna, one of the greatest of the Hindu sages, who practised in both Buddhism and Christianity as well as in his own Hindu tradition and received profound realizations on all three paths, favoured the metaphor that the soul can 'become the sweetness' or can 'taste the sweetness', i.e. enjoy the bliss of unity and the bliss of contemplation. He did not elevate one above the other.

But this still has not fully resolved the question of individuality. Does all sense of personal identity disappear, along with all the memories and experiences that formed part of this sense of identity? Does the individual as a self-aware being cease, effectively, to exist? Do we go through the process of birth, life and death, with all the challenges, struggles and lessons that come through being an individual and through possessing self-awareness, for these things to have no ultimate meaning? If so why go through all this? If we go back to the state from which we arose, then why leave this state in the first place? If I am pressed for an answer I would repeat the point made earlier, namely that our lives are a work in progress, and the way in which we live these lives contributes something of value to the whole.

There is an old saying that our lives are gifts *from* God, and that what we make of them are our gifts *to* God. A diamond sparkles through the diversity of its many facets, so perhaps our lives, ultimately purified by our long journey through the realms of form and of formlessness, become analogous to these facets, each with its individual contribution to make to the whole. The process of creation is infinite and eternal, and we are part of how this creation happens. Another useful analogy sometimes employed is that rather as each small part of a hologram contains the whole hologram – albeit with fainter colours – so each individual is a fainter reflection of the whole of creation. Eternity indeed in a grain of sand.

Journey's end

If this is so, is there anything beyond the Seventh Plane, is our journey like climbing a mountain only to see distant peaks shining ever further on the horizon? How can any of us know? And indeed why should we ever think in terms of limits? If the Divine, the Absolute is limitless, then our finite attempt to conceptualize its nature will never be more than partial. Perhaps there are still more distant peaks even after the Seventh Plane, and perhaps there are not. Either way, as the mystics assure us, all will be well, and to live and be part of divine creation is the greatest of all blessings.

REFERENCES

Bander, P (1972) *Carry on Talking*, Colin Smythe Ltd: Gerrards Cross

Barrett, Sir W (1986) *Death-bed Visions*, Aquarian Press: Northamptonshire (first published 1926)

Beard, P (1980) *Living On*, George Allen & Unwin: London

Begley, S (2007) *Train Your Mind, Change Your Brain*, Ballantine Books: London and New York

Boyd, J N and Zimbardo, P G (2006) 'Constructing time after death: the transcendental – future time perspective', In L Storm and M A Thalbourne (eds.) *The Survival of Human Consciousness*, McFarland: Jefferson NC and London

Broad, C D (1962) *Lectures on Psychical Research*, Routledge & Kegan Paul: London

Brown, R (1971) *Unfinished Symphonies: Voices from the Beyond*, Morrow: London and New York

Bucke, R M (1956) *Cosmic Consciousness: A Study of the Evolution of the Human Mind*, Dutton: New York

Budge, Sir E A Wallis (1972) *Egyptian Magic*, Routledge & Kegan Paul: London and Boston (first published 1899)

Buhlman, W (1996) *Adventures Beyond the Body*, HarperSanFrancisco: New York

Cardoso, A and Fontana, D (2004) 'Proceedings of the First International Conference on Survival of Death with Special Reference to ITC'. ITC Journal Publications: Vigo, Spain

Chadwick, H (1966) *Early Christian Thought and the Classical Tradition: Studies in Justin, Clement and Origen*, Oxford University Press: Oxford

Cherrie, M (1987) *The Barbanell Report* (edited by Paul Beard), Pilgrim Books: Norwich

Chéroux, C, Fischer, A, Apraxine, P, Canguilhem, S and Schmit, S (2005) *The Perfect Medium: Photography and the Occult*, Yale University Press: New Haven and London

Christie-Murray (1988) *Reincarnation: Ancient Beliefs and Modern Evidence*, Prism Books: Bridport, Devon

Cockell, J (1993) *Yesterday's Children*, Piatkus: London

Conze, E (1967) *Buddhist Thought in India*, University of Michigan Press: Ann Arbor (originally published by Allen & Unwin)

Corazza, O (2008) *Near-Death Experiences: Exploring the Mind-Body Connection*, Routledge: London and New York

Crookall, R (1964) *More Astral Projections*, Aquarian Press: London

Crookall, R (1974) *The Supreme Adventure*, James Clarke (2nd edn.): Cambridge

Crookall, R (1978) *What Happens When You Die*, Colin Smythe Ltd: Gerrards Cross

Cummins, G (1935) *Beyond Human Personality*, Ivor Nicholson & Watson: London

Cummins G (1984) *The Road to Immortality*, Pilgrim Press: Norwich (originally published in 1935)

Dalai Lama, His Holiness the (2000) *The Transformed Mind*, Hodder & Stoughton: London

Dante, Alighieri (2008) *Divine Comedy: Hell, Purgatory, Paradise*, (trs. H Longfellow, originally published 14th century), Arcturus: London

Darling, D (1995) *After Life: In Search of Cosmic Consciousness*, Fourth Estate: London

Delacour, J-B (1974) *Glimpses of the Beyond*, Dell: New York (German edition published by Econ Verlag under the title *Aus dem Jenseits* Zuruck, translated by E B Garside)

Doidge, N (2007) *The Brain that Changes Itself*, Penguin: London and New York

Dowding, Lord H C T (1945) *Many Mansions*, Rider: London

Dowding, Lord H C T (1951) *The Lychgate*, Rider: London

Evans-Wentz, W Y (1960) (ed.) *The Tibetan Book of the Dead*, Oxford University Press: Oxford

Fate Magazine (1996) *Psychic Pets and Spirit Animals*, Llewellyn Press: St Paul MN

Fenwick, P and Fenwick, E (1995) *The Truth in the Light*, Hodder Headline: London and New York

Findlay, A (1931) *On the Edge of the Etheric*, Psychic Press/Headquarters Publishing Company: London

Findlay, S (1961) *Immortal Longings*, Victor Gollancz: London

Fiore, E (1980) *You Have Been Here Before: A Psychologist Looks at Past Lives*, Sphere Books: London

Fisher, J (1990) *Hungry Ghosts*, Grafton Books: London

Fodor, N (1933) *Encyclopaedia of Psychic Science*, Arthurs Press: London

Fontana, D (1991) 'A responsive poltergeist: a case from South Wales', *Journal of the Society for Psychical Research* 57, 823, 385–403

Fontana, D (2005) *Is There an Afterlife?*, O Books/John Hunt: Ropley, Hants

Forman, R K C (1991) *Meister Eckhart: Mystic as Theologian*, Element Books: Rockport MA and Longmead, UK

Fox, M (2003) *Religion, Spirituality and the Near-Death Experience*, Routledge: London and New York

Gallup, G, Jnr (1983) *Adventures in Immortality*, Souvenir Press: London and New York

Gauld A (1971) 'A series of drop-in communicators', *Proceedings of the Society for Psychical Research* 55, 204 (whole issue)

Gauld, A and Cornell, A D (1979) *Poltergeists*, Routledge & Kegan Paul: London

Glaskin, G M (1974) *Windows of the Mind*, Hutchinson/Arrow: London

Glaskin, G M (1978) *Worlds Within*, Hutchinson/Arrow: London

Goswami, A (2002) *The Physicist's View of Nature*, Springer: New York

Goswami, A, Reed, R and Goswami, M (1993) *The Self-Aware Universe: How Consciousness Creates the Material World*, Putnam & Sons: New York and London

Govinda, Lama Anagarika (1977) *Creative Meditation and Multidimensional Consciousness*, Mandala/Unwin: London

Grant, J (1956) *Far Memory*, Arthur Barker: London

Grant, J and Kelsey, D (1969) *Many Lifetimes*, Gollancz: London

Grey, M (1988) *Return from Death: An Exploration of the Near-Death Experience*, Arkana: London and New York

Greyson, B and Flynn, C P (1984) (eds.) *The Near-Death Experiences: Problems, Prospects and Perspectives*, Charles C Thomas: Springfield Ill

Greyson, B and Bush, N E (1992) 'Distressing near-death experiences', *Psychiatry* 55, 95–110 (reprinted in Bailey, L W and Yates, J (eds.) *The Near-Death Experience*, Routledge: New York and London)

Groff, S (1975) *Realms of the Human Unconscious: Observations from LSD Research*, Viking Press: New York

Groff, S (1994) *Books of the Dead: Manuals for Living and Dying*, Thames & Hudson: London

Guirdham, A (1980) *Paradise Found: Reflections on Psychic Survival*, Turnstone Press: Wellingborough

Harlow, S R (1968) *A Life After Death*, MacFadden-Bartell: New York

Harrison, T (2008) *Life After Death: Living Proof*, (revised edition), Saturday Night Press: London

Hart, H (1959) *The Enigma of Survival*, Rider: London

Hay, D (1987) *Exploring Inner Space*, (rev. edn) Continuum Intl: London and Oxford

Head, J and Cranston, S L (1977) *Reincarnation: The Phoenix Fire Mystery*, Julian Press: New York

Heath, P, and Klimo, J (2006) 'What the channelled material of suicides tells us about the afterlife', In L Storm and M A Thalbourne (eds.) *The Survival of Human Consciousness*, McFarland: Jefferson NC

Heathcote-James, E (2003) *After-Death Communication*, Metro: London

Hick, J (1976) *Death and Eternal Life*, Collins: London

Hyslop, J (1918) *Life After Death: Problems of the Future Life and Its Nature*, Dutton: New York

Jahn, R and Dunne, B J (1987) *Margins of Reality: The Role of Consciousness in the Physical World*, Harcourt Brace Jovanovich: New York

Jansen, K L R (2001) *Ketamine: Dreams and Realities*, MAPS: Sarasota Fl.

Jung, C G (1960) Psychological commentary in W Y Evans-Wentz (ed.) *The Tibetan Book of the Dead*, Oxford University Press: Oxford

Kardec, A (1989) *The Spirits Book, Brotherhood of Life*: Albuquerque NM (first published 1885)

Keen, M, Ellison, A and Fontana, D (1999) 'An account of an investigation into the genuineness of a range of physical phenomena associated with a mediumistic group, in Norfolk, England (the Scole Report)', *Proceedings of the Society for Psychical Research*, 58, 220, 150–452 (whole issue)

Koenig, H G, McCullough, M E and Larson, D B (2001) *Handbook of Religion and Health*, Oxford University Press: Oxford and New York

LaGrand, L E (1997) *After Death Communication: Final Farewells*, Llewellyn: St Paul MN

Larsen, C D (1927) *My Travels in the Spirit World*, Tuttle Publishing Co.: Rutland Vermont

Lati Rinbochay, and Denma Lochö Rinbochay (1983) *Meditative States in Tibetan Buddhism* (Zahler, L and Hopkins, J trans.), Wisdom Publications: London

Leonard, G (1937) *The Last Crossing*, Cassell & Co: London

Lester, R (1952) I*n Search of the Hereafter*, Harrap: London

Litvag, I (1972) *Singer in the Shadows: The Strange Story of Patience Worth*, Macmillan: London and New York

Lodge, Sir Oliver (1916) *Raymond or Life and Death*, Methuen: London

MacGregor, G (1992) *Images of Afterlife*, Paragon House: New York

Manning, M (1974) *The Link*, Colin Smythe: Gerrards Cross

Mateu, L (1999) *Conversations with the Spirit World*, Channelling Spirits Books: Los Angeles

Matson, R (1975) *The Waiting World*, Turnstone: London

Miller, S (1998) *After Death: How People Around the World Map the Journey After Life*, Touchstone: New York

Monroe, R (1972) *Journeys Out of the Body*, Souvenir Press: London

Moody, R (1975) *Life After Life*, Bantam Press: New York

Moore, Vice Admiral W Usborne (1915) *The Voices*, Watts & Co.: London

Morse, M and Perry, P (1990) *Closer to the Light*, Villard Books: New York, Souvenir Press: London

Morse, M and Perry, P (1995) *Parting Visions*, Piatkus: London

Muldoon, S and Carrington, H (1987) *The Phenomenon of Astral Projection*, Rider: London (first published 1951)

Myers, F W H (1903) *Human Personality and its Survival of Bodily Death*, Longmans Green: London (reissued 1992 by Pelegrin Books)

Neiman, C and Goldman, E (1994) *Afterlife: the Complete Guide to Life After Death*, BCA/Labyrinth: London and New York

Oaten, E (1938) *That Reminds Me*, Two Worlds Publishing: London

Osis, K and Haraldsson, E (1986) *At the Hour of Death*, Hastings House: New York

Parnia, S (2005) *What Happens When We Die*, Hay House: London

Pauchard A (1987) *The Other World*, Pelegrin Trust/Pilgrim Books: Norwich (transcribed by 'MJ')

Peterson, R (1997) *Out of Body Experiences*, Hampton Roads: Charlottesville VA

Pfeiffer (ed.) (1921) *Meister Eckhart*, Watkins (2 Vols.): London

Playfair, G (2008) *This House is Haunted: An Investigation of the Enflield Poltergeist*, Souvenir Press: London (originally published 1980)

Pole, W Tudor (1984) *Private Dowding*, Pilgrim Books: Norwich (originally published 1917)

Price, H H (1995) *Philosophical Interactions with Parapsychology: The Major Writings of H. H. Price on Parapsychology and Survival*, Macmillan: Basingstoke, St Martin's Press: New York

Radin, D (1997) *The Conscious Universe*, HarperEdge: San Francisco

Radin, D (2006) *Entangled Minds*, Paraview/Simon & Schuster: New York and London

Ring, K (1984) *Heading Towards Omega*, William Morrow: New York

Ring, K (1990) 'Shamanic initiation, imaginal worlds, and light after death' in G Doore (ed.) *What Survives? Contemporary Explorations of Life After Death*, Tarcher: Los Angeles

Ring, K (1999) *Mindsight*, William James Center for Consciousness Studies: California

Roberts, J A (2002) *Quiver of Guides and Poltergeists*, Tegai Publishing: Bangor

Sabom, M (1982) *Recollections of Death: An Investigation Revealing Striking Medical Evidence of Life After Death*, Corgi/Transworld: London

Sabom, M (1998) *Light and Death: One Doctor's Fascinating Account of Near-Death Experiences*, Zondervan: New York

Saltmarsh, H F (1938) *Evidence of Personal Survival from Cross Correspondences*, Bell & Sons: London

Sheldrake, R (1983) *A New Science of Life*, Granada: London and New York

Sheldrake, R (1988) *The Presence of the Past*, Collins: London and New York

Sheldrake, R (1990) 'What survives?' in G Doore (ed.) *What Survives? Contemporary Explorations of Life After Death*, Tarcher: Los Angeles

Sheldrake, R (1999) *Dogs that Know When Their Owners are Coming Home: And Other Unexplained Animal Powers*, Hutchinson: London

Sherman, H M (1972) *You Live After Death*, Ballantine Books, 3rd edn.: New York (originally published 1949).

Sherwood, J (1964) *Post-Mortem Journal*, Neville Spearman: London

Sherwood, J (1969) *The Country Beyond*, Neville Spearman: London

Shinners, J (2007) (ed.) *Medieval Popular Religion: A Reader*, Broadview Press (2nd Edn.): Toronto

Smith, A (1962) *Primer for the Perplexed*, Dent: New York

Smith, S (2000) *The Afterlife Codes*, Hampton Roads: Charlottesville VA

Solomon G, and Solomon, J (2006) *The Scole Experiment*, Campion Books (revised edn.): Waltham Abbey, Essex

Stead, E W and Woodman, P (eds.) *The Blue Island*, London (no publisher given – available for download at www.spiritwritings.com/Blue Island.pdf)

Stevenson, I (1974) *Twenty Cases Suggestive of Reincarnation*, University of Virginia Press: Virginia

Stevenson, I (1987) *Children Who Remember Past Lives*, University of Virginia Press: Virginia

Storm, H (2000) *My Descent into Death*, Clairview Books: London

Suzuki, D T (1979) *Mysticism: Christian and Buddhist*, Mandala Books/Unwin: London and Boston

Swedenborg, E (1966) *Heaven and Hell*, Swedenborgian Society: London (first published in the original Swedish in 1758)

Thomas, Rev. Drayton (1936) *In the Dawn Beyond Death*, Psychic Press: London (re-issued 1960)

Thurman, R A F (trans.) (1994) *The Tibetan Book of the Dead*, Thorsons: London

Turvey, V N (1969) *The Beginnings of Seership*, University Books (American edn.): New York

Van Lommel, P, Van Wees, R, Meyers, V and Elfferich, I (2001) 'Near-death experience in survivors of cardiac arrest: a prospective study in the Netherlands', *The Lancet*, 358 (9298) 2039–2045

Wallace, A (2007) *Contemplative Science*, Columbia University Press: New York and Chichester UK

Wambach, H (1979a) *Reliving Past Lives*, Hutchinson: London

Wambach, H (1979b) *Life Before Life*, Bantam: New York

Ware, Father Kallistos (1979) *The Orthodox Way*, Mowbray: London and Oxford

Watts, A (1954) *Myth and Ritual in Christianity*, Thames & Hudson: London

Webster, K (1989) *The Vertical Plane*, Grafton/Collins: London

Weiss, B (1988) *Many Lives Many Masters*, Warner Books: New York

Wickland, C A (1978) *Thirty Years Among the Dead*, Spiritualist Press: London (originally published in 1924)

Wilkins, Sir H and Sherman, H M (1971) *Thoughts Through Space*, Frederick Muller: London (first published 1951)

Willin, M (2007) *Ghosts Caught on Film: Photographs of the Paranormal*, David and Charles: Newton Abbott

Williston, G and Johnstone J (1988) *Discovering Your Past Lives*, Aquarian Press: *Wellingborough*, Northants

Wilson, I (1988) *The After Death Experience*, Guild Publishing: London

Wydenbruck, Countess Nora (1946) *The Para-normal:Personal Experiences and Deductions*, Rider: London

INDEX